NICE COMPANIES
FINISH FIRST

NICE COMPANIES
FINISH FIRST

WHY CUTTHROAT MANAGEMENT IS OVER— AND COLLABORATION IS IN

PETER SHANKMAN
with KAREN KELLY

palgrave
macmillan

NICE COMPANIES FINISH FIRST
Copyright © Peter Shankman, 2013.
All rights reserved.

First published in hardcover in 2013 by PALGRAVE MACMILLAN® in the United States—a division of St. Martin's Press LLC, 175 Fifth Avenue, New York, NY 10010.

Where this book is distributed in the UK, Europe and the rest of the world, this is by Palgrave Macmillan, a division of Macmillan Publishers Limited, registered in England, company number 785998, of Houndmills, Basingstoke, Hampshire RG21 6XS.

Palgrave Macmillan is the global academic imprint of the above companies and has companies and representatives throughout the world.

Palgrave® and Macmillan® are registered trademarks in the United States, the United Kingdom, Europe and other countries.

ISBN: 978-1-137-27915-6

Library of Congress Cataloging-in-Publication Data

Shankman, Peter.
Nice companies finish first : why cutthroat management is over—
and collaboration is in / Peter Shankman.
    p. cm.
    1. Corporate culture. 2. Organizational effectiveness. 3. Leadership. 4. Customer relations. I. Title.
HD58.7.S4763   2013
658—dc23

2012035386

A catalogue record of the book is available from the British Library.

Design by Letra Libre, Inc.

First PALGRAVE MACMILLAN paperback edition: June 2014

10 9 8 7 6 5 4 3 2 1

Printed in the United States of America.

CONTENTS

ACKNOWLEDGMENTS AND DEDICATION

This book wouldn't have been possible without some help from some wonderful people out there.

First off, it's been a pleasure to have a writing partner on this journey, Karen Kelly. For all the things that my ADHD prevented me from doing, you stepped up time after time. Thank you.

Thanks to Bill Wagner and Rick Rudman at Vocus, Inc. You may not know this, but when you bought my company, I watched how you both worked for a bit, and that gave me the idea for this book. Well, that, and because I believe most bosses in the world should be a little nicer, a little more like the both of you. So thanks for that.

As always, much love to Mom and Dad, as well as Alan, Carol, and Amy, for your constant "How's the book going?" notes. Thanks also to Ty for listening to me complain when I got stuck.

Meagan Walker, my assistant and personal lifesaver for more than four years now, don't ever leave me. You're the port in my professional storm.

Finally, this book is dedicated to my amazing wife Kira, without whom my life would be empty, and our soon-to-be-born (right around the time this book comes out) first child. May your actions allow you to finish first in everything you ever do.

1

WHAT'S SO GREAT ABOUT BEING A NICE GUY?

"Be the change you want to see."

—Gandhi

Not too long ago I was standing in line at the airport waiting to check in. The whole experience of flying has been severely downgraded over the last 20 years, from glamorous and exciting to dismal and depressing, not to mention inconvenient and uncomfortable. So I wasn't really all that surprised to see the person in front of me, a normal-looking guy in a suit, throw a tantrum that would put an overly tired, sugar-infused three-year-old to shame. I know you've seen this before: Tantrum Guy wasn't getting his way. Didn't the airline rep know who he was? He should get the seat he wanted. Why wasn't he getting bumped up to business class? Everyone at the airline was a jerk. He was important. He had to get to a VIP meeting. The ticketing agent remained stoic during his unconstrained tirade.

> The most powerful leaders are almost always the role models for the change they seek.

We've all been witness to this kind of embarrassment at one time or another. I just shook my head, rolled my eyes, and briefly made eye contact with the agent. None of my fellow passenger's perceived problems was the fault of the agent, who was, of course, just doing her job amidst her own problems, like bills to pay, an annoying supervisor, or a kid on the verge of becoming a teenager. Still, Tantrum Guy didn't give a thought to any of this. To him, the agent had ceased to be human and instead became the vessel into which he poured all of his petty aggravations and frustrations. In reality, the agent continued to be patient and polite, and then she dispatched him as quickly as possible, all while he continued to whine and complain loudly.

"Well. . . . That sucked." I smiled as I got up to her. "I give you a lot of credit for letting him leave with his teeth." I grinned. "I hope your day gets better from here."

"Thank you, Mr. Shankman," she said as she smiled back. "How can I help you today?"

"Oh, I just need to check in, and with any luck, you won't have to deal with any more idiots of that caliber today."

And with that I was upgraded to first class.

Lesson number one: it pays to be a nice guy. Second: always stand behind a pompous ass whenever possible. Your niceness will be thrown into dramatic high relief.

> There's no way to institutionalize or "corporatize" niceness—it comes from the top person and permeates a place.

Let me tell you another story. I have a colleague who worked for a big corporation more than 20 years ago. That's a lifetime in working terms. She had a boss who could be very cutting—it was a management style that defined her, in fact. She pitted the members of her team against each other so that they often worked at cross-purposes. That was bad enough, but the offhand insults she threw at them were perhaps the most harmful of all. Words sting. Especially when they come from a supervisor.

At any rate, one day my colleague was asked to re-do a report done by a person in another department. She took on the challenge and did her best. "I felt very proud of that report," she said. "But when I showed it to my boss, instead of sensing my pride and thanking me at least for the effort, she said, 'You're not that good at this,'" referring to the analysis my friend had put into the report. "I carried those words with me for 20-plus years," my friend told me. "They were always in the back of my mind, even though I had gone way beyond that job." In fact, today she is a very successful consultant whose insightful analysis of markets is in huge demand.

"One day I was minding my business, and my old boss wanted to friend me on Facebook," she said. "I thought, okay, I'm curious. But I couldn't help but be reminded of the way she had treated me—and my colleagues. I posted the revelation of how awful it had been on my page, without mentioning her name. Even though she recognized herself and apologized, it seemed very hollow to me. What was more interesting was the many responses I got from Facebook friends—how it resonated. So many of us have been hurt by bosses, people who we want desperately to trust." This isn't an unusual story—carrying around the toxic spew of a bad boss affects too many people. The difference is that nowadays we have the chance to announce it to the world.

These incidents got me thinking. I'm a serial entrepreneur, a CEO, and an avid student of brands and marketing, so I tend to look at life from a business perspective. It occurred to me that in business, one of the most demonized populations around (with good reason), nice people, actually can and do finish first despite the conventional wisdom that says you have to be a cold, uncaring bastard to succeed in the corner office. In other words, more and more, nice guys *do* win. That's why I always take the first meeting and try to have five minutes for someone. You never know where that first meeting will lead, and you never know what can be accomplished in those five minutes. Understand—this doesn't mean I get taken advantage of. I always tell people (with a smile): "Happy to answer a question you might have, but don't ask me to write your marketing plan for you." There's a big difference between being nice and being taken advantage of. Good leaders know this and work accordingly.

If you look under the hood of successful companies, you'll find that they are made up of people working together in an atmosphere that is conducive to civility and good cheer. There's no way to institutionalize or "corporatize" niceness—your HR department is never going to come up with a management structure that magically creates a collegial atmosphere. It *has* to come from the top, and from there it will filter down through managers, supervisors, staffers, and so on (the same can be true of a negative atmosphere).

I'm not just talking about making your business the top in its sector, exceeding sales expectations, or making boatloads of money. First of all, nice CEOs can (and do) make great business *and* plenty of dough (Richard Branson at Virgin, Shantaul Narayen at Adobe, and Kenneth Chenault at American Express, to name a few). Nice guys have a constant competitive advantage over their nasty counterparts, as illustrated by my airport story. Versions of that same scenario play out every single day, and not just in terms of the CEO who yells at his assistant, but also with the CEO who refuses to answer shareholder questions, who cheats employees out of bonuses, or who treats stakeholders and the community like dirt.

There's a growing body of research indicating that bad bosses hamper productivity, which results in smaller profits and lost business. University of Florida researchers found that people who work for abusive bosses are more likely to arrive late, do less work, and take more sick days even though they may be physically fine. Wayne Hochwarter, an associate professor of management at the Florida State University College of Business, and his colleagues interviewed more than 700 people from a variety of industries about the treatment they received from their managers. The results were dismal:

- 31 percent reported that their supervisor gave them the "silent treatment" during the year.
- 37 percent said that their supervisor failed to give credit when due.
- 39 percent noted that their supervisor didn't keep promises.
- 27 percent told the researchers that they had discovered that their supervisor made negative comments about them to other employees or managers.
- 24 percent reported that their supervisor invaded their privacy.
- 23 percent indicated that their supervisor blamed others to cover up mistakes or to minimize embarrassment.

According to the researchers, this kind of employee–manager abusive relationship resulted in a workforce that "experienced more exhaustion, job tension, nervousness, depressed mood and mistrust." These workers were also less likely to take on additional tasks, such as working longer or on weekends, and were generally less satisfied with their jobs. Also, employees were more likely to leave if they were involved in an abusive relationship than if they were dissatisfied with their pay—proving the old maxim that people quit bosses, not companies.

Ultimately, strong leadership is the most important competitive advantage companies have—it comes first, before technology, finance, operations, and everything else. "Nice" CEOs and managers are the best leaders: run better companies, attract innovative and more loyal employees, get into legal and regulatory trouble far less frequently (if ever), have better relationships, get more done, and are even healthier than the bad guys. And I can prove it.

In this book, I identify nine "nice" characteristics. I talked to dozens of CEOs, entrepreneurs, and other leaders who embody these traits and practice them actively to very profitable effect. My hope is that I can encourage a whole new generation of CEOs, managers, and entrepreneurs to embrace their inner nice guy (or gal) and make it the hallmark of their business life. Who knows? Maybe a few Tantrum Guys will even change their attitudes.

Read on. Let's learn about these traits—Do you identify with any of them, either positive or negative? Do you see yourself as a "good" CEO or a "bad" CEO? More important, how do your employees see you?

One last story: I was sitting in a meeting with a CEO a few years ago when an administrative assistant walked in, caught her foot on a piece of rug that had curled up, and went down like a lead balloon, taking with her about 200 collated but not stapled pages. The CEO, in his thousand-dollar suit, jumped up and sat on the floor with the admin, picking up and re-collating papers for the next ten minutes. We all joined in as well. End result? No harm, no foul, and no injury to anyone's pride. That CEO had his company acquired for about $600 million last year.

Not bad for a guy sitting on the floor collating papers.

2

THE NINE WARNING SIGNS OF A HOPELESS JERK

"Some cause happiness wherever they go; others, whenever they go."

—Oscar Wilde

Are you reading this book because your nasty side gets the better of you some of the time or maybe all of the time? Or is it because you want to make sure the leadership of your company is in the best shape to take it into the next decade? Or is it because there could be something wrong at the top and you can help fix it—or find another company that better suits your needs? All good reasons for coming along on this ride (and a fun ride it will be). Welcome to the fray.

Before we get into the positive traits that make leaders shine, let's spend a little time on the traits that make for bad leaders, the bastards that drive employees crazy, the ones who take too many unacceptable risks that are bad for shareholders or who behave in ways that are simply bad for the image of the business. Here are the warning signs that a hopeless jerk could be running your company—or, if you're willing to take a good look at yourself, the warning signs that *you* may be the jerk (or that you are perhaps heading in that direction). Think of the following as a diagnostic checklist.

1. **Know-It-All Dictator:** The top dog doesn't leave room for disagreements out of a sense of personal insecurity, arrogance, or both. The loyalty of the few cronies he or she has is built on fear, and so isn't authentic friendship (hey, it also means those cronies could stage a coup at some point and throw him or her out). This often results in a dulled level of commitment and enthusiasm on the part of other employees and partners who may stop telling the truth or even start lying just to avoid the boss's wrath. Backbiting among the executives and managers can become common and public. This makes for a highly stressful workplace and results in an increased rate of no-shows, as well as an accelerated turnover rate.

2. **Uninterested in Feedback:** Feedback, often called "360 Feedback," allows employees to give and receive confidential, anonymous feedback on a wide range of workplace issues both to and from the people who work around them, including supervisors, peers, and direct reports. Leaders who don't care what their staff thinks of managers and of the leadership itself aren't interested in solving personnel problems or, for that matter, in enhancing relationships that are working. You don't have to hire expensive outside consultants to run a feedback program—but the best leaders usually have some system in place that measures and codifies how they're perceived in terms of management weaknesses and strengths.

3. **Takes Sides Unfairly and Openly:** Don't you love it when the boss lets some people go home early while

others (you, maybe) are stuck behind to clean up the
mess? How about those whispery, gossipy sessions you
see him or her having with a colleague behind a barely
closed door? I'm sure we've all watched those before
with a "WTF" look on our faces. Or, worse, you see that
stock options, bonuses, and perks are unfairly linked to
completely subjective performance reviews. "If you can
see performance is rewarded and it's transparent and
everyone gets a chance to earn that too, then preferential
treatment is fine. If special treatment is not transparent
and not clear, you are creating a very bad political
situation," says Robert Sher, head of CEO to CEO, an
executive consulting firm.

4. **Wasteful or Out-of-Whack Use of Resources:** Leaders
   who allocate budgets to business units or departments
   based on favoritism and power centers rather than actual
   business needs, innovation, or performance are wasting
   talent, plain and simple. How long do you think it will
   take for that to bite you back?

5. **The Desert Island Boss:** A leader with nonexistent
   stewardship doesn't care about local community, doesn't
   hire local workers, and doesn't participate in local
   community outreach. Moreover, he or she engages in
   products or services that don't contribute positively
   to the environment or the community either locally or
   globally.

6. **Wants a Castle in the Sky:** Empire builders believe that the
   more people they manage and the bigger the budget, the
   greater the chance they'll get promoted. This management
   style often results in ugly turf wars and can destroy
   productivity, innovation, and workplace harmony. It can
   also lead to bloated management, with too many layers

within and between departments. Nothing gets done because people are too busy figuring out protocol and checking off boxes on lists. Good luck trying to beat the competitor in that castle. They'll be coming in through the windows.

7. **Talks Too Much, Does Too Little:** You can't just talk about great ideas; you have to implement them, too. When you're all talk and no action, rank-and-file employees become disillusioned. They start blogs or online businesses selling flea market scores, or they write screenplays on company time because you're too busy listening to yourself pontificate. Your managers waste budgets and time on report after useless report. In short, teams become fragmented, and people lose interest. "Don't leave someone in place who can't deliver," says Sher.

8. **Thinks Adversaries Work Better than Teams:** Bosses who foster the idea that every person is in it for himself or herself interfere with a sense of camaraderie or esprit de corps. Telltale signs are argumentative and heated meetings where everyone is either sending barbs across the table or checking their Droids. The key criterion for decision making is *What's in it for me?* After a while, the answer for many workers becomes all too apparent: nothing.

9. **Constant Cycle of Crisis:** You know, it may be true that you should never waste a good crisis, but it's also true that creating and maintaining a crisis mentality is a recipe for burnout. When your people spend most of their time putting out fires, eventually there's nothing left to save. Crises may feel exciting, but they are a brain and energy drain.

The first step in fixing a problem is admitting there is one. How much of your company (or yes, even yourself) do you see in the above examples? Let's get busy removing these warning signs of a hopeless jerk from the earth. Keep reading.

3

TRAIT #1

Enlightened Self-Interest

"The future has no shelf life. Future leaders will need a passion for continual learning, a refined, discerning ear for the moral and ethical consequences of their actions and an understanding of the purpose of work and human organizations."

—Warren Bennis

"The Universe tends to unfold the way it should."

—Harold and Kumar Go to White Castle

The trait that underpins all other nice traits is enlightened self-interest—the act of doing something that benefits you and your constituents, whoever they may be. It's such a crucial concept because it represents the ultimate combination of human nature and strategic thinking. Human nature, because self-interest alone is a powerful force; many prominent psychologists and psychiatrists claim that our everyday decisions are based on what's good for us. Even when we comfort a crying baby, experts argue, we are essentially making ourselves feel better, because it upsets us to hear the wails. Strategic, because it's only when we see tending to the needs of others as helping ourselves that society becomes more civil and utter chaos doesn't ensue—hence, enlightened self-interest. It's a concept as old as the hills and a clear theory for success in today's transparent world.

Scottish philosopher Adam Smith noted the benefits of enlightened self-interest as early as 1776 in his *Wealth of Nations*.

Smith's purpose in writing the book was to topple the popular ideology of the mercantilist system, which held that wealth was fixed, like a pie with only a certain number of pieces, and that the only way to prosper in this finite world was to hoard gold and tax products from abroad. In other words, wealth could not be created from individual effort or without forcibly taking it away from someone else. The idea was that nations should sell their goods to other countries but buy nothing in return. As a result, countries became mired in rounds of retaliatory tariffs that choked off international trade, not to mention stifled individual and group prosperity.

The core of Smith's thesis was that man's natural tendency to look out for number one results in prosperity. Boiling his principles down to essentials, Smith believed that a nation needed three elements to bring about universal prosperity, and one of them was enlightened self-interest. In Smith's famous example, your local butcher doesn't supply a great rib eye based on altruistic intentions, but because he makes a tidy profit by selling you a nice piece of meat. If the cut he sells is low quality or rotten, you're not going to want to do business with him. It's in the butcher's interest to sell you a good piece of meat at a price you're willing to pay: you and the butcher both benefit from the transaction. Smith believed that long-term thinking would keep most businesses from taking advantage of customers—those who did would eventually shutter their doors. For those who have a tendency to cheat no matter the illogic of it, government regulations would prevent or punish wrongdoers.

It was a Frenchman, of all people, who later observed the American tendency to practice enlightened self-interest. In his 1835 book *Democracy in America,* still widely read and assigned in college classes today, Alexis de Tocqueville described how Americans voluntarily joined together in associations (including businesses) to further the interests of the group, thereby serving their individual interests. Tocqueville sums up the concept of enlightened self-interest this way:

> The Americans, on the contrary, are fond of explaining almost
> all the actions of their lives by the principle of interest rightly
> understood; they show with complacency how an enlightened
> regard for themselves constantly prompts them to assist each
> other, and inclines them willingly to sacrifice a portion of their
> time and property to the welfare of the state. . . . I do not think
> upon the whole that there is more egotism amongst us than in
> America; the only difference is, that there it is enlightened—
> here it is not. Every American will sacrifice a portion of his private interests to preserve the rest; we would fain preserve the
> whole, and oftentimes the whole is lost. Everybody I see about
> me seems bent on teaching his contemporaries, by precept and
> example, that what is useful is never wrong. (*Democracy in
> America,* Chapter 8: The Americans Combat Individualism by
> the Principle of Interest Rightly Understood)

Tocqueville's observations were significant because of his own social and political milieu. A political thinker and historian, he was educated at a time when France was marred by political revolutions and the iron hand of centralized government. By the time the French Revolution began, his parents had been thrown in jail, and his maternal grandfather and one of his aunts had been sent to the guillotine. At the time, the French aristocracy and political elite saw any kind of political association as dangerous to the state. In America, local liberties triumphed, encouraging individuals to form groups that defined and addressed their needs and aspirations. Tocqueville said that without the freedom to participate via association, people would be hesitant to join together for common goals. As a result, a fluid civil society would have a hard time surviving. He was talking about the survival of the democratic process—but likewise, businesses that are run like dictatorships don't have as much of a chance to excel and grow as those that are run by leaders who create an atmosphere where employees feel they are working toward and can benefit from a common goal.

One wonders what Smith and Tocqueville would make of the high-profile Enron, WorldCom, Tyco, Computer Associates, and Bernie Madoff scandals (to name but a handful) that have made headlines over the past several years. At the truest, most basic root of all of these outrageous examples of corruption is the loss of enlightenment in the self-interest equation. What makes leaders think it is in their self-interest to use their power and influence at the expense of their constituents, shareholders, or clients? Greed, blind ambition, a thirst for power, certainly. For some it might be a hole in their personality, a lack of empathy—the same character flaw that allowed them to compete and win aggressively is also the one that serves their downfall, and the higher this person rises, the bigger the shockwave when that flaw finally comes to light. And let's be very clear—unlike the 1950s, when information could be hidden, adapted, and then finally doled out so there was no blowback, this is 2012. Those days are *over*, and they're never, ever returning. The past 20 years have proved that information will always flow down the quickest and most available open channel, and in the age of Facebook, Twitter, TMZ, and anonymous email accounts, the chances of any CEO successfully hiding anything for any amount of time is virtually nil.

Also remember: if you hide something that can affect you, your company, your bottom line, or your shareholders, it has to be hidden *forever*. Even if the Internet and immediate communication didn't exist, that would still be almost impossible to do. Enlightened self-interest needs to begin with transparency, a topic that we'll touch on in depth later in this book.

The most basic responsibility that CEOs and other leaders have is the promotion of the welfare of their clients, workers, shareholders, and stakeholders. This is a huge task, since these groups often have competing interests. These leaders, like all of us, want to succeed, be noticed, win public praise and admiration, get promoted, earn raises, and get offered better jobs at competing firms. All good in my book—but how do you get all the benefits of leadership without becoming a total asshole, not to mention a guaranteed future guest of some minimum-security prison? Enlightened self-interest.

GOODNESS KNOWS

The key to enlightened self-interest in terms of leadership is to think, as Adam Smith suggests, in terms of the transactional benefits of what you do on a daily basis. If the transaction isn't going to benefit the business and its clients and employees over the long term—and *you* as a result—then don't do it. Simple enough, yes? That's why it puzzles me that some leaders fall back on coercive tactics ("Do what I say or you're out") and peer pressure ("Why don't you come in as early and stay as late as Mary does?") as management techniques, since in the end they ultimately backfire and distance leaders from those around them. I'm not saying there's not a time for a CEO to say, "We're doing it my way because I'm the boss and I'm making the final decision"—that's not coercive or bullying, that's being a CEO and making the sometimes unpopular decision based on your years of experience. Bullying means that the self-interested team member or customer will eventually take their business elsewhere. Moreover, a feared leader is an isolated leader—once distanced from staff or clients, he or she can quickly start to make selfish decisions that ultimately come back to bite him or her in the butt. You can make beneficial decisions and lead your company to greatness without resorting to third-grade schoolyard tactics. Too many CEOs don't realize that.

Consider Al Dunlap, former CEO of Sunbeam, who earned nicknames like "Chainsaw Al" and "Rambo in Pinstripes" thanks to his gleeful appetite for massive job cuts in his organizations. According to *Forbes* magazine, Dunlap had become a Wall Street hero after firing thousands of employees at Scott Paper and selling the company to Kimberly-Clark at a huge profit. When he moved to Sunbeam in 1996, its stock doubled in six weeks, increasing his wealth by almost $60 million. In short order he slashed half of Sunbeam's 12,000 employees and trimmed its product offerings. In January 2002 he was fined $15 million for falsely reporting performance. He also managed to plunge the company into near bankruptcy before it canned him.

People were afraid of him for good reason. Dunlap's dark side was very black indeed. He told his first wife he wanted to know what human flesh tasted like, and he dissed both his parents' funerals by failing to show up. His staff did what they could to avoid the verbal abuse he famously let loose at the drop of a hat. As John A. Byrne noted in his book about Dunlap, *Chainsaw: The Notorious Career of Al Dunlap in the Era of Profit-at-Any Price,* "At his worst, he became viciously profane, even violent. Executives said he would throw papers or furniture, bang his hands on his desk, knock glasses of water off a table, and shout so ferociously that a manager's hair could lift from his head by the stream of air that rushed from Dunlap's screaming mouth."

Dunlap also used coercion and peer pressure, to say the least, on employees. For instance, everyone's performance was compared unfavorably to employees at other companies he ran. And if employees didn't hit their numbers, he would tear them apart and threaten them: "I have thousands of résumés from people who would work here for free." It didn't take long for people to just stop telling him the truth. Dunlap's cruel ambition and ruthless disregard for the humanity of his employees, and his utter selfishness, led to the accounting scandal and his dismissal.

There will always be Dunlaps, unfortunately. But on the plus side, social media makes it much harder for these characters to sustain themselves than in the past. Just Google "Christian Bale and freak out" or "Mel Gibson and rant" and you'll see that in today's world everyone has become a potential broadcaster, making it much harder for "Rambo"-type CEOs to stay in power, because someone, at some point, is going to hit "record" on their Droid and then hit "publish to YouTube" when they've finished recording the outburst. Such retaliation might even be worth the fallout for the employee posting the incriminating video—what does getting fired from a job matter if it relieves a company and its shareholders of a liability like a lousy CEO? So this is not an "if" scenario. It *will* happen. Boards can't afford to have Dunlap-style leaders who can be "outed" and tweeted about instantaneously. It would be very easy for customers to be so insulted by such behavior that they would simply start to buy another brand of blender or toaster. And what senator or billionaire wants to watch the CEO they've been buddying up to for months or years go off on a tirade about a religious group or a political affiliation? It's happened countless times already, and it will continue to for the foreseeable future, at least until a generation that's raised to assume there's always a camera present gets old enough to get into power.

The paradox, however, is this: we all still want to succeed, compete, and win. A leader who practices enlightened self-interest employs six strategies that are key to ensuring both personal success and integrity. He or she

1. Creates a system in which the leader feels secure but is also accountable. He or she is confident enough to say, "I made a mistake" when he or she screws up;
2. Appeals to workers' own enlightened self-interest by investing in individual growth and development, which makes all transactions globally beneficial;

3. Consults early with those who will be affected by big decisions;

4. Seeks counsel and listens carefully and rarely acts in a vacuum;

5. Expects the truth and responds with dignity even if the truth isn't pretty; and

6. Reacts in a way that won't add insult to injury even when things are at their worst, and thereby deprives public sharks of content that could further hurt the company.

I found some interesting leaders in tough industries who exemplify enlightened self-interest in ways that have paid off big-time for both them personally and their companies and employees. The ways in which they strategically run their companies, manage employees, and make decisions prove that even if you're competing with the big guys on a daily basis, you can keep your sanity, self-respect, and principles and still come out ahead. What's interesting about the following examples is how some of the smallest innovations or practices these leaders engage in provide the most valuable insights for those who want to develop their own enlightened self-interest.

A MINDFUL EGO

Michael Tompkins is president and general manager of Miraval Arizona Resort and Spa. Miraval is a top-rated high-end destination retreat situated on 400 acres in the Santa Catalina Mountains in northern Tucson, Arizona. If running the place sounds like a dream job, you're halfway there. Who wouldn't want to work in such a stunning environment, helping people relax and find their Zen? Keep in mind, however, that the hospitality business is fraught with many sensitive issues that stem from dealing with the public on a daily basis. When people come to a spa like Miraval, they're often coming with more than just their physical baggage. They may be in search of a respite from a demanding job, recovering from a loss, or just in need of a temporary escape. Whatever the reason, every person who walks through the door may not automatically have a smile on his or her face. Still, Michael couldn't be happier to take on the challenge every day. "I have a hard job, but I can't wait to get here each morning," he says.

> "When I make a big decision, I think, how is this going to impact the guest experience first, how will the staff be affected, and finally, what's it going to do to me?"
>
> —Michael Tompkins

A lot of Michael's enthusiasm for his job is a result of his leadership approach, which encapsulates the idea of "life in balance," one of the retreat's core philosophies of living mindfully. "Everything we do encourages our guests to live in the present moment, conscious of the unique intersection of mind, body, and spirit," he says. "Our human side comes before the business side." Like the butcher in the Adam Smith story, Michael wants to provide the best transactional experience for customers that he can, and in hospitality, it makes perfect sense to accentuate the human side. The human side of Miraval *is* its business side.

The practices and programs he's instituted at the resort have paid off for both him and the resort. Since he started at the spa in 2007, he's earned three promotions and the financial rewards that go with them. In part, the rewards have come because he's elevated the already well-respected Miraval brand. In 2011, Miraval hauled in more awards from readers of travel magazines and websites than at any time in its 16-year history. Accolades include top-ten rankings in various categories in Trip Advisor, *Travel*

+ *Leisure,* and *SpaFinder,* and the spa made the "Gold List" of Condé Nast's "world's best places to stay" for 2012. Those tributes translate directly to the bottom line, including an amazing 30–50 percent rate of return for repeat customers.

Since hospitality is about people, it pays for Michael to invest in both staff and guests by making them all feel as if they are part of the brand. "Our staff and hosts have taken ownership of [the] brand as if it's their own. I can go to our employees and say, here's where we are at in financials this month and here's where we need to be. I need to count on you to cut back where possible, use paid time off wisely, and generate new ideas for revenue growth. I usually get 30 ideas in 24 hours because people feel vested in making the business successful," he says.

Michael's ability to connect with employees also benefits the business and his role as GM. "The typical GM, especially at a luxury facility, would be Sir or Mr. to employees," he says. "At Miraval, everyone calls me Michael. I make an effort to get to know employees and their families. I had dinner two nights ago at a Ritz Carlton and I asked the server who the GM was. She had no idea." She told Michael that the GM very rarely made an appearance, and when he did, there was no connection between him and the front-line staff. "That's the conventional way of running a hotel. But if I am present here, I have to reach out to employees. Because of that, Miraval is more family oriented, and the staff is very connected to each other." Employee turnover is lower, and customer service exceeds expectations, at least according to guest comments.

Miraval's rate of return is also up because of an innovative customer loyalty program called Authentic Circle. Based on the number of days a customer comes over their lifetime, they can reach one of three tiers that go from Step to Run to Fly. After three visits, a guest becomes a Step member and earns perks like extra dollar credits for services, a gift, or even a meeting with Michael when he travels in their city. How many CEOs do you know who have dinner with an individual customer who isn't necessarily a "big spender"? So enthusiastic are customers about the program that they strive to up their visits to achieve rewards. "I have even had Step members come back four times in one year so they can get to the Run level. It's very beneficial for the business," says Michael.

Michael has also seen the advantage of Facebook and other social media for him and the business. "When I started my personal Facebook account I had maybe 100 friends and I now have 700 friends," he says. "Many are business peers or Miraval guests. At first I'd get advice along the lines of not mixing personal with business, but right off the bat I said, why not? I am the same at home as I am at work and I don't think I'm doing anything detrimental to business. What I found is that many guests become friendly and feel they know me. When I posted that my dog had to have surgery, I actually received three gifts from guests who were FB friends. Social media has essentially solidified the relationship I have with guests, which is very different from the traditional hotel model that has always worked off customer service once in the door but never blending personal and professional lines. Ultimately, what has been a very enriching experience for me personally has been very good for the brand. Customers take Miraval very personally, and being 'personal' friends with me on Facebook enhances that feeling and creates more brand loyalty."

Michael also uses social media strategically to build business, particularly during the economic downturn of 2008. "We used to use flash sale sites, and we still do occasionally," he says. "We would put special offers on the sites, essentially loss leaders, as the sites get a hefty portion of the sale. But it would get people in the door who we could build into repeat customers. Now we put those same special offers on the Miraval Facebook fan page, which we've built in one year from 1,500 to 23,000. Fans can book special deals directly through us via social media and we actually make money on the discounted bookings." One social media sale that the spa ran only to Facebook fans resulted in several *hundred* overnight bookings, essentially proving to Michael that he could eliminate flash sale sites from the business model. "Miraval is a healthier business now, and all the money we make is directly tied to better engagement of our guests. It's key in terms of the repeat model," he says.

Building up employees as personalities has burnished Michael's reputation as a manager and contributed to the bottom line. "Our latest cookbook is an example," he says. "The number one request we get from guests is a cookbook." *Mindful Eating* by Miraval is the result. "It's spectacular. I wrote the mindfulness section, and the staff worked on recipes. When I learned the book process, I thought, why don't we do more of this? I had a meeting with the programs team and said, if you guys can get book proposals done, let's make you a brand and get you out there. Books help paint Miraval in a professional manner, they give us a whole other level of credibility." The result? Miraval scored a deal for six more books from its publisher, Hay House, all done by Miraval staffers. "It gives the employee writing the book added income and it broadens our brand and profile in a very professional and appropriate way."

The decision to get into the book business was almost a no-brainer for Michael. But not every decision is so easy—and this is where enlightened self-interest gets seriously important. "When I make a big decision, I think, how is this going to impact the guest experience first, how will the staff be affected, and finally, what's it going to do to me?" says Michael. "When making tough decisions that impact other people's lives, I try to follow my heart—otherwise I'll end up remorseful. I try to sit and think about it ahead of time, and if it is a huge decision, I'll take a vacation for a couple of days so I am capable emotionally and physically of handling any fallout. One thing I never do is to leave *after* a tough decision is made. I want to understand how people feel and be available to them, because they ultimately want to be heard. If they feel that way, then they are more often than not okay with decisions even if they disagree with [them]," he says.

Shedding old notions of keeping proprietary information close to the vest has helped Miraval as well. "The conventional wisdom is that you don't share with peers the positives that have happened on the property because it gives you the upper hand," Michael says. "I feel the more people know about our successes, the better off we are. I am on an international speaking tour, and sharing our success makes others want to be part of it. It's not done in a bragging kind of way, but in a helpful way: here's what we did and here's how it impacted us. Competitors can jump on the celebration of our business. I did a talk in Vancouver, British Columbia, to other spa directors, and some people said to me, 'Why are you giving your competitive edge away to people who are striving for the same dollars?' But to me it's the bigger pie theory. Three people booked at Miraval after my talk. Sharing our successes and failures with colleagues in the industry has helped the bottom line in an amazing way."

Michael also encourages his staff to go to other spas and check out the facilities, service, and amenities. "We choose people at the end of the year who receive the trades we get from other hotels and spas," he says. "It's a well-earned vacation, but they learn about how other high-end places do it. A housekeeper making $11 an hour takes her husband to one of the best resorts in the country. That's a wow to them, but on top of that, they see how competitors operate and treat the guests, because they go as a guest. When they return to work, they carry it with them to their jobs. Or they understand that the Miraval way is really very special. It just creates a level of enthusiasm and excellence on the job that makes us an award-winning spa. And the employee ends up with a deeper connection to what can seem like mundane tasks. They see how important they are to the guest experience."

The most resonant example of Michael's enlightened self-interest is how he makes room for personal well-being—something not all CEOs are especially known for or even willing to talk about. "We're a wellness-based company, so I need to be an example of it," he says. This concept is enlightened self-interest to the core—finding balance in life couldn't be more self-sustaining. It reminds me of what we're told during the in-flight safety lecture—always put on your air mask before helping someone else. Take care of yourself first, and you can care for others so much more effectively.

"There are a few things I do regularly," Michael says. "I resolutely walk my dog every day; what I have found is that because my dog anticipates that walk, even if I am tired that day, if I see her wagging her tail, it changes my whole day. So I begin my day with that walk, drop her off, and get in another three and a half to four miles on my own before heading to work." He also participates in Miraval's athletic offerings, not only to check out the actual event, but also to benefit personally from the experience of it. "I most recently invited a member from the security department on one of the Miraval hikes. It gives employees a chance to see me as a real person and not just a guy behind the desk concerned about financials." Plus, they both get in a good workout. His home, he says, has also been designed to feel as spa-like as possible "to create a sense of retreat when the workday is done," he explains—"and that included putting Miraval bed linens on my bed. Investing in little things has transcended positively into my work." Namaste.

THE CURRENCY OF CARING

As CEO and member of the board of directors of supply chain finance firm PrimeRevenue (PR), PJ Bain is, like all top executives, responsible for the company's overall corporate direction and performance. But he's also an entrepreneur at heart and keeps that spirit alive in the way he manages the company. In 1996, PJ founded Inspired Solutions, an award-winning firm that grew to be the largest reseller of Exact Software in North America. His record at PR is impressive. Since joining the company in July 2009, the heart of the economic downturn, the company has doubled revenues twice, with a growth rate approaching 200 percent over 30 months. "I think the board is happy," he says with a grin. "One of the reasons I decided to join PrimeRevenue was because of the board of directors, which includes CEOs of public companies, entrepreneurs, and successful venture capitalists. I'm always looking for what the next big thing in our industry is, and they're focused on the same thing, so it's a good fit."

> "I'm a big believer in personal development too, since so much of what we do is on display for our customers to see."
> —PJ Bain

The company's online platform based on cloud computing connects very large supply chains for global multibillion-dollar companies like Volvo, Kohl's, and Whirlpool. These companies have thousands of suppliers, and PR helps them speed up the flow of money through the chain by finding banks to pay the invoices early and collect on them when they are due in 120 days (or whatever the negotiated cycle is). "Banks will say, I like Volvo's risk in the market at this price, and then sell the invoice for a slight discount based on the risk assessment. It's much cheaper money for the bank. We source the cheapest funding and create efficiency and reduce the cost for Volvo while also giving the supplier ready access to cash," PJ explains.

It's a very cool business model, but PR is competing with some big guns in this space, including Citibank and JPMorgan Chase—two of the biggest banks in the world. "Typically, when we get in front of the CFO of a company like Volvo or Sears—and we are comparatively tiny next to those competitors—we have to explain who we are and why they should go with us as opposed to two very big operators. We always talk about our ability to do what we do better and faster. It also means we have to prove it every single day. We have to do everything as if the company's life depends on it, because it does," says PJ. "If we are issuing payment instructions for a $100,000 million transaction, it has to be perfect, but the same effort has to be put into a single slide during a PowerPoint presentation. Ultimately, the details represent the entire company to the marketplace. They also represent me."

PJ has instituted some innovative ways to sustain the trajectory of the company. "We have an internal portal that allows for information sharing," he says. "We try to pick several ideas generated from that program every quarter or half year and pursue them. I'm a big believer in personal development too, since so much of what we do is on display for our customers to see. We like to send employees to Toastmasters to become better speakers, and we encourage the staff to seek out mentors. We have soft dollar and hard dollar investments in that associated with each employee. The one thing we ask of them is to share what they learned from any educational experiences with their colleagues."

Another program PR offers is a book club, which focuses on team-building books. "Right now we're in the middle of *Crucial Conversations: Tools for Talking When Stakes Are High*. Once a month we bring in lunch and one person will facilitate the meeting, where we talk about the ideas in the book we've been reading." Everyone gets involved in the discussion, not just those in the home office. The company holds book club meetings globally by videoconference with its offices in London, Paris, Frankfurt, Prague, Melbourne, and Hong Kong. "It's important that everyone in the company is speaking the same language and understands and shares information and ideas," says PJ, who attends the book club meetings along with his employees. It also creates a feeling of community among far-flung employees.

Anything PJ can do to get people across departments together, like the book club and PrimeRevenue University, a program in which employees learn about the company philosophy, helps build bonds that make the company work to its fullest potential. "When the programmers, who work at computer screens all day, spend a full day with someone in sales and they have a conversation, there is a bond that forms. Now they know each other personally and they aren't just throwing something over the wall at a stranger. Maybe it sounds altruistic, but at the end of the day we see it helps people perform more effectively," he says.

It's essential for the company to foster this kind of camaraderie and mutual understanding, because PJ is very serious when he says growth is the crucial factor in the company's sustained success as well as his own. It's growth that puts a lot of pressure on staff, and there is always risk involved, risk that it won't work, that people will get burned out—any number of things can happen when you're constantly looking to expand. "I seek out mentors with more experience than me but who share common values," he says. "I also come from an engineering background, so I gather as many data points as possible and chop them up to see if a decision is a good one before making it. Once you've made the decision, we have to get people on board; otherwise, it won't work."

When the company decided to open an office in Brazil, PJ had lengthy discussions about the timing of the move with his board, peers, and staff. "Brazil is a very difficult country for us to go into," he says, recognizing that a certain level of pain and discomfort would be inevitable in developing the service and sales teams in Brazil, a country with regulations that make Sarbanes-Oxley look like a children's book. "We all huddle together and the service team presents their case as to how much pain will be on their people who are already overloaded and so on. We try to accommodate for that. But we also realize that the opportunity is so big that we want everybody to understand how big a play it is, how important it is for the company—for employees. Everyone gets buy-in because they have the opportunity to express the good and the bad from their point of view. It's up to me to explain how the move is aligned with our corporate objectives." PJ did the convincing, and the company plans to go into Brazil sooner and more aggressively. "Bottom line, every day my job is on the line, so I have to do what's right for the company."

SHARING THE MARKET

Byron Lewis Sr. is the founder and CEO of UniWorld Group, the oldest multicultural advertising agency in the United States. His story is an ideal example of enlightened self-interest—Byron saw an untapped market in which he could build a business and fill a need at the same time. UniWorld started back in 1969, when there was little interest in the black consumer market, the primary minority population at the time. "The ad business was closed to minorities, and women, for that matter," says Byron. It was a situation that went both ways—ad agencies didn't employ people of color, and they really didn't advertise for them either. Consider too that in 1969, the only media outlet for minorities was *Ebony* magazine. The only other way that African Americans found out about the news in their community, including consumer news, was through buzz or word of mouth.

In order for his fledgling company to succeed, Byron had to think outside of the conventional methods for finding employees. "There were very few people available who had training in a mainstream company who also understood the market," he says. "I had to find creative individuals and at the same time prove to potential clients that there was a minority consumer market worth pursuing."

Today that's different, of course. Byron says that based on results from the 2010 census, consumers of color, including African Americans, are the fastest-growing population in the country. "They have rising income and a grasp of technology, both of which are a basis for growth in this industry," he says. "I have always felt one of the benefits of working here and working in this marketplace is that you quickly have to understand digital space, strategic thinking, entrepreneurship, strategy, and salesmanship in order to succeed." This is even more crucial today, since the industry has grown in complexity, and the economic downturn that began in 2008 meant that UniWorld had to do more with less—clients give them fewer resources to work with but want as much or more in return.

In the beginning, Byron had to, out of necessity, hire people who lacked experience working for major ad companies but who brought other experiences that would be an asset to solving problems. Creative people were at the top of the list. "They are the lifeblood of our company and need special consideration," he says. He learned that listening to people was both in his own best interest and in the best interest of his company and clients. "The group would talk and maybe argue, and ultimately we would agree on what was a good solution to a particular client's issue. It's a policy we continue today, to respect opinions. Sometimes they're ridiculous and outrageous, and sometimes they're just what the doctor ordered. That's why sharing ideas has become the framework for our continued success, even though we're larger now and have three different offices."

In order for any company to last as long as UniWorld has, and to grow besides, its leader also has to be comfortable with risk. "Almost every business decision we make is a risk because many of the companies we work with don't have a true understanding of ethnic communities in terms of consumer behavior," says Byron. He describes a solution-based campaign his firm did for 7-Eleven stores in the 1990s. "The desire was to find a way to maintain school attendance of the urban 7-Eleven customer in the Dallas and Houston region, who were largely Hispanic and African American. Most of these kids had to work, and that could make it difficult for them to be consistent students." UniWorld came up with a program called College Pass. It enabled these kids to work at various 7-Eleven outlets and gain an extra financial benefit if they maintained school attendance: the company would match their earnings by putting [them] into a bank account at a Latino or ethnic bank in the community."

In order for the program to work, UniWorld and 7-Eleven had to build relations with local community organizations and the mayors. The client felt that there was a great deal of risk and had no experience with this kind of thing. College Pass was successful and met the goals—attendance went up, and UniWorld was able to track benefits and sales in 7-Elevens in the areas that ran the program. The other aspect was a tremendous amount of positive media coverage for 7-Eleven. "We were also able to track the economic value of that. It was a solution based specifically on what I learned from employees about what was important to them and what we could do to make parents of youngsters more interested in 7-Eleven. My employees understood the background of these customers," says Byron.

Turnover is, according to *Ad Age,* "rampant" in the ad business, and if you're a small company, losing even one valuable person can be a blow. It's in your interest to retain the good ones and keep churn to a minimum. Byron's secret sauce of sharing information helps manage that too. "We have a top tier of people who have been here for 38 years, and several who have been here for 25 or more in the financial, media, and creative departments because we continue to learn from each other and these people feel their contributions have value," he says. "I encourage loyalty and effectiveness by giving respect to employees' ideas. When people see their ideas being used, they feel their careers are being enhanced."

To keep younger employees interested and inspired (and Byron says some do leave to go to major corporations, with a major leg up from having worked at UniWorld), the company has pioneered a lifestyle division of younger people who work at a grass-roots level on music and fashion trends. This helps keep the established firm on the cutting edge of pop culture innovation. "It also brings younger people in contact with older, senior staff, which is good for both of them," he says. "The young people bring refreshing insights. Yet there is a distinct need and requirement that experienced senior people work closely with younger employees so they get the attention and training necessary to function at a high level. It is an absolute requirement of senior people, because we still have to find creative people who have to learn on the job since there are not enough younger people of color working in the ad industry to begin with.

"We have most recently created an initiative, UniWorld Urban Bloggers Collective, where we bring in people who represent decision makers at the major television broadcast and print mediums who talk about what's going on in those realms and who encourage conversation in areas of political or entertainment interest.

They talk about issues that affect women and that have to do with the gay and lesbian segment," says Byron. These conversations enable UniWorld to know more about its clients' customers—information they share with them. "We can tell clients very frankly how their brands are perceived and used by customers. It provides a good, honest look at the likes and dislikes of consumers, and a very current way to keep up with what is going on in the world and how we can attach their products to the right strategy."

Byron still has lively exchanges with his employees and clients every day. It just doesn't get old for him, even though he could probably delegate a lot of that listening to others. "My door is always open," he says. "Talking to people has become a source of joy for me because I love the interchange. I love that people feel free to approach me with ideas. My people are very interesting, and that's important for clients. You can only work well if you have a good day-to-day rapport with each other."

SUMMARY OF KEY POINTS

Leaders who practice enlightened self-interest

- See business as a series of positive transactions that have benefits for both sides;
- Weigh the benefits for each side to make sure everyone is getting "market share"—and is aware of it;
- Understand what decisions will be beneficial all the way around—to them and to their constituents;
- Engender loyalty and get employees on their side through respect and listening, not through fear or coercion;
- Seek counsel when making decisions;
- Consider potential outcomes and consequences before acting;

- Are aware that any negative or damaging action they take in the "heat of the moment" can be leaked to the world, which negatively adds to the situation;
- Cultivate authenticity;
- Take proper care of their well-being and maintain balance in their lives;
- Expect excellence from employees and give support so it can be achieved;
- Promote, support, and reward great employees because it's good for business and good for the boss; and
- Expect honesty and practice it.

4

TRAIT #2

The Accessibility Factor

A friend of mine—I'll call him Joe—told me about getting in an elevator with the president and CEO of the large corporation he worked for, which produced and sold entertainment media to "average" consumers. The two were in the company headquarters in a Midtown Manhattan high-rise. This fellow was Joe's boss's boss's boss's boss, or something like that. At least five other executives stood between my friend and the head honcho. Except in the elevator: it was just the two of them. Like someone being confronted with a celebrity, Joe was tongue-tied at first, but eventually he forced out a "Hello, how are you?" After the guy nodded in Joe's general direction, my friend continued to try to break the silence with something about the Yankees—he couldn't quite remember what. The CEO nodded again, smiled thinly, and then reverted to a straight-ahead blank gaze.

When Joe got back to his office, he related what had transpired in the elevator to his boss, Frank. "You actually *talked* to him?" Frank said incredulously. "Sure, why not, we were in the elevator together, riding up 42 floors," said Joe. "You're not supposed to address him," Frank told him. "Everyone knows that." "I thought he was the president of the company," Joe told me, "not the king."

A couple of years later, the company's stock had fallen, the board was unhappy with the CEO, and he was out. I'm not saying the guy was canned because he refused to talk to Joe in an elevator. Other things were in play—the company was late to the game in a couple of areas where it should have been innovating. It had also made some bad merger and acquisition decisions. But the leader's attitude toward Joe (and others) was part of his problem as a manager. Leaders who behave as if they're royalty or above it all tend not to do well—it's especially incongruent when they run a middle-market consumer company. These types of leaders are not inclined to understand the pulse of the business, the customer, or what's happening in the culture. Besides, that kind of behavior is simply obnoxious—the fact is, the CEO *isn't* royalty. If you can't be friendly to someone who works for you, works his ass off for you, in fact, then maybe you don't deserve to have anyone working for you.

A CLEAR WARNING

Inaccessible, aloof CEOs can run successful businesses for a while, but in the long run, they make bad leaders. They are rarely effective as visionaries, managers, administrators, or communicators. Would it kill a CEO to have a conversation with an employee in the time it takes to travel 42 floors? It wouldn't. These kinds of leaders turn off employees by making them feel less than human and unimportant, and they are sending a message: you don't count. This is dangerous on many levels.

Even worse, arrogance and distance are often accompanied by narrow-mindedness and an unwillingness to listen to other people. Insulating yourself from the people who make the business run is, without question, one of the best ways to start making bad decisions. This is true even if the boss has other managers and executives in place who are accessible to those outside the executive bubble. I've discovered two things about inaccessible leaders: 1) they send a bad message to employees, and morale declines; and 2) the CEO's decision making suffers by not having a pulse on the business. He or she should not depend on seconds and thirds in command to let him or her know what's going on. CEOs have to find out for themselves—get out there and smell the air. CEOs and leaders who are accessible have happier workforces and make better decisions about their companies.

Of course, there is a matter of degree of accessibility, not to mention the importance of at least appearing to be available. You may know people who you think are aloof but who do well. In fact, I have a colleague, a publisher, who tells me he wants to be like his counterpart at another company: "I wish I could be like X, he never returns phone calls."

First of all, I can't imagine wanting to be like someone who doesn't return phone calls, but second, he doesn't really grasp the dynamics of this guy. I happen to know that the man doesn't return *his* calls, or the calls of a bunch of other people who the publisher has determined are not essential to his business. But this is also a leader who engages his employees, especially his top editors and writers. He's accessible to the people he has identified as essential and important. There's the difference.

I understand that CEOs can't be accessible to everyone every minute, but they have to engender a spirit of accessibility among their most important constituents—employees being number one. So think twice before you say that CEOs don't have to have great personal skills or an ability to engender a feeling of accessibility to be successful. It's fine if you're not the chatty type. Being accessible is not necessarily defined by backslapping, chummy-style banter. You have to be true to your personality, and you have to be authentic. The leaders who do the best job of creating a feeling of accessibility have four major characteristics that stand out:

1. Shows commonsense respect and openness for and with colleagues, direct reports, and rank-and-file workers—no matter how distant they are on the company flow chart.
2. Creates an environment that makes for easy cross-pollination between people, no matter what department or rank they hail from.
3. Establishes a feeling of workplace equality, where everyone's job is valued as prestigious and important to the bottom line.
4. Shares as much information with as many people in the company as possible as a sign of respect, inclusion, and transparency.

The following five leaders exemplify these qualities and are considered accessible, respectful, and transparent by both their peers and their employees.

SEND THE RIGHT MESSAGE

James "Jamie" Sprayregen is recognized as one of the country's outstanding restructuring lawyers and has led some of the most complex Chapter 11 filings in recent history, including those for United Airlines, Zenith Electronics, A&P Supermarkets, Conseco Insurance, and dozens of other very large companies. The

National Law Journal chose him as one of the "Decade's Most Influential Lawyers."

> "You have to put yourself in a position of being lucky. If you are getting along with others, it seems your odds are greater for getting lucky."
>
> —James Sprayregen

So you'd think a guy like that would have a pretty big head—lawyers aren't known for their modesty to begin with. But according to Jonathan Friedland, a former colleague from the law firm Kirkland & Ellis, that's anything but the case. "He is, perhaps, the single most sought-after lawyer in the country for that sort of work. He is also universally respected for just being a good guy. I used to be a partner at Kirkland & Ellis, and Jamie was the senior partner. He was everything you would want in a boss," says Jonathan. "I started as a gun-shy, less than confident associate and left with the view that I could accomplish anything if I put my heart and mind into it. I credit Jamie with a lot of my growth."

What is Jamie's secret for engendering that kind of respect among reports and peers? "The first thing you have to understand is that law firms are not like regular companies where there is a CEO. It's more diffuse than that, so you can't lead by pretending to be 'command and control.' The only way to do it is if you lead in a way that people are willing to follow, and that means they have to like and respect you and vice versa," he says.

One of the ways Jamie shows respect is in his attitude toward employees—something that any CEO, including those who don't like to talk to underlings, can take a lesson from. "In a law firm, the inventory goes down the elevator every night," says Jamie. "We sell people and that's what we need to be successful—people who are happy, respectful, and want to do the job every day. That's what we nurture. It's a never-ending balance in a competitive atmosphere. I tell young associates what goes around comes around, and keeping that in mind is not a bad way to conduct yourself. I am a fan of treating people right. I don't care if they work for me or are selling a newspaper down the street. It's not that hard. I don't believe in stress taking over your behavior. We're paid to be calm in the storm, so if we are getting stressed out, we are not being good to our clients—emotions in this area should be theatrical and not actual."

Aside from giving and expecting respect and kindness, even in the high-pressure and competitive world of a law office, Kirkland & Ellis offers mentoring, educational programs, and individual department learning that brings together senior people and newbies. In this way, all young associates get to know the higher-ups on a one-on-one basis. The junior people learn more, and they also forge relationships that last a lifetime and help them in their careers. The idea is that the firm is not only helping clients, it's building the kind of lawyers who will keep the firm going into the future. Even if associates leave for other firms, they take with them important lessons about how to conduct themselves, and they spread good feelings about the firm as they travel in their careers.

VOCUS ON AVAILABILITY:
BUILD IT AND THEY WILL COME

Rick Rudman runs Vocus, a $100 million software PR firm in Maryland. He's taken accessibility to heart by being available not only to his executives but to his rank-and-file workers as well— and in a whole new way. He built a state-of-the-art office and made it into—literally—a small town where small-town relationships flourish. "People feel very comfortable stopping me on the 'street,' and I feel the same," says Rudman of the 100,000-square-foot warehouse he turned into a small town complete with coffee shops, a music store, barbershop-themed meeting rooms, and a "park" where it never rains, along with lots of places people can get some thinking done away from their desks but without leaving the premises.

> "We spend one third of our lives at work. Anything we can do to help make it enjoyable is worth it."
>
> —Rick Rudman

In other, more traditional companies, Rick says, you have to go out to Starbucks or other local coffee shops to talk to colleagues or get some peace and quiet. That time out of the office is often the most productive, innovative time between workers. "I hear that consistently from people," he says, "where they have to leave the office to get work done because they are always being interrupted. But here you never have to leave—you can find solace right in town."

The environment creates new interactions among employees, no matter what their position, just by allowing them to get a cup of coffee or lunch. "When you go to Main Street, you are naturally running into people and talking to them, and that's exactly why we built this facility. To create an environment where you would run into people that you might not run into in a typical workday, if you just sat in your office," says Rick. It's a social environment within the work environment that reinforces productivity, curiosity, and mutual respect.

"Sure, when someone asks me why there are no Tootsie Rolls in the kitchen, I think, *really* . . . but the return on investment is too great to worry that much about the occasional inappropriate or misdirected question," says Rudman. Since building the structure, Vocus has seen both productivity and profits rise. "I also think that sort of comfort level is only partly due to the office structure. Vocus tends to skew to a lower age demographic; our average age is 31 and I'm 50, so I skew toward the top. So a lot of newer, younger employees for good and for bad have different expectations of boundaries. So the net-net is greater because of our set-up," he says.

The idea for a town-office started more than 15 years ago with Rick's co-founder. "We were brainstorming in our hole-in-the-wall office about what an ideal office would look like. A couple of years ago we were getting ready to make a move, and because of the huge rise in social media, I started thinking about this concept of a social office and how it could help connect people and the flow of ideas and information. I thought, it's time to try to pull our idea off."

It took almost a year to create the actual structure, and then there were at least another four months of planning. Vocus's office is based on the planned community in Florida called Seaside and something called New Urbanism. "I had gone to Seaside a number of times for vacation and was impressed," says Rick. "Once I decided to do the town-as-office thing, I took a lot of inspiration from the way Seaside is organized."

Rick also formed an employee committee that met throughout the process and provided a feedback loop. "We had reps from all departments to share what was going on and update employees. We also posted a drawing of the new office, and we put a pad of sticky notes next to it, and the thing got covered with hundreds of messages and a lot of the ideas made their way into the final building.

"I knew in the first week it was going to exceed my expectation. It's cool because to get a cup of coffee, you have to get up and leave the office and pick one of the three or four coffee shops in the facility. I'll run into people there, and then check the

Vocus Community College to see what class is going on." Aside from the educational and social opportunities Vocus provides, in 2007, the company implemented two standing committees. One is called It's All About You, an employee wellness program with a budget to determine activities that are purely fun and healthy. They have yoga classes and fitness instruction. They built an 18-hole golf course that ran through the office. Not only does this promote health, but it also promotes interaction between people in the company who may not meet in the course of a normal day—no pun intended. In this way, junior people can meet senior people on a whole different turf, forge relationships, and perhaps find champions, sponsors, and mentors along the way.

"We also implemented an It's Not All About You Committee," says Rick. It focuses on philanthropic activities such as Water for People. "We have literally participated in dozens of nonprofit activities that come from employee suggestions," he says. It's another way of bringing people together from different reporting groups and departments. "I am a big believer in making Vocus a great place to work. If we invest in our people and in making everyone happy, there is a big payoff. Even if there wasn't, I would do it anyway."

SAFE HARBOUR

In just 12 months, Shandon Harbour, the CEO of SDA Security in San Diego, California, completely revamped the company's culture from one that was rigid and unengaging to one that is collaborative and encourages independent thinking and risk-taking. With great attention to detail, she has also implemented several minor improvements that have made a big difference in the overall morale of employees. For example, SDA removed the soda vending machine, going to an honor system, and added a popcorn machine to the break room. It was a small, but significant, way of saying "We trust you" to everyone. A more elaborate project was an Amazing Race program, in which employee teams scooted around the company's neighborhood in a fun scavenger-like activity.

"What can I do that will get people motivated to be at work and engaged, but that's inexpensive?" she asked herself when she took over the company in 2007. "I'm not running a huge company; I can't bring babysitters in or other perks large companies offer. We are in a business where the culture is driven by first responders, fire, police, and it can be bureaucratic—a 'high-and-tight,' crisp atmosphere, which is appropriate most of the time. But that doesn't mean work can't be fun or that the work itself is not enjoyable."

So she got out of her own comfort zone to try to do something different, especially during lunchtime. "We did ping-pong March Madness with teams in costumes. We had brackets and a cheering section. At the start of it, there was a lot of nervous chatter, 'Oh, she wants us to wear costumes,' but you know, I had technicians come in Hawaiian shirts and cowboy hats called Blazing Paddles, and it was fun. We did a book club in the summer. The energy these things created was phenomenal. People became charged— and it takes an hour from the rut and routine. It costs very little and the payback is huge," she says.

Shandon's message of "We all work here together" has indeed made a difference. "It's much easier to hold the reins tightly and keep it at a comfortable jaunt. So far the numbers have shown me it's the right way to go," she says. Sounds ridiculous? Ridiculously profitable. Since her initiatives began, turnover has decreased from 29.83 percent to 14.07 percent, absenteeism has decreased by 17 percent, and reoccurring monthly revenue has increased by 13 percent. SDA Security was also nominated for the 2011 Workplace Excellence Award.

"SDA is a third-generation family business," says Shandon. The company started in the 1930s with her grandparents and then was led by her father from the 1960s through the 1990s. "As society changed," she says, "we had to change to meet the needs of employees. The Internet has also altered the security world tremendously, and the rate of having to make decisions—good decisions—has increased." Shandon says that in the old days, before she took over, her father would make every decision, no matter how small. "When I took over, there was a general paralysis, because no one would do anything until they got my okay. I had to empower employees to make their own judgments."

That was harder than it looked, because having one person make every choice was so ingrained in the culture. "If my dad took a vacation, everything would grind to a halt and the office would become very unproductive without the king to say what was what," she says. That affected everyone, employees and customers. If a client or worker can't get something handled, they feel powerless—and unimportant. "You can't run a business like that today. It was also a tremendous burden on me to have that many decisions, including how much coffee to buy for the kitchen, running through my desk on a daily basis," she says.

Shandon started at the company in 2003 in human resources, then did four years as general manager. "I was laying a lot of groundwork for how I would run the office by working closely with as many employees as I could," she says. "As my dad approached 65, we knew he would get out of the business. I have no background in security other than it was a family thing. I came in and I saw many people who were scared to make decisions—but who have a tremendous amount of knowledge and experience that I did not have when it came to the security business." Shandon needed those people to feel empowered enough to make their own decisions and to take control of their jobs in an autonomous way—she also wanted their feedback, guidance, and information.

"I needed their expertise," she says. "I didn't want anyone to give me a yes answer because they thought that's what I wanted to hear. It was a process of making sure they knew I wasn't wearing a crown, but that I was a member of the team. It took a while before everyone felt confident that I really wanted them to start making decisions as well as any changes they saw that were necessary in their own processes."

> "If employees see that I'm willing to incorporate fun into work, they may also think, 'Hey, if she can do an Amazing Race during lunch hour, maybe she wants to see us suggest changes in process.' And they're exactly right."
> —Shandon Harbour

It certainly wasn't easy. Shandon went through a challenging two-year phase with her right hand, a VP who was excellent at operational efficiencies. "You would get all the right numbers from him, but he led by fear and intimidation and lots of fist pounding and no jumping rank. Talk about inaccessible. The operations department almost collapsed because no one wanted to stick their heads out," recalls Shandon. "I had to let him go. It was the right thing to do." Once he was gone, the fear was gone, and everyone in the department stepped up to the plate. People with hidden talents bubbled up to the surface. "It's amazing how letting that one person go totally changed the dynamic of the company," she says.

That firing gave Shandon and others in the company momentum to make more changes. "We decentralized decision making so that managers are signing off on the activities of their departments," she says. "When you give people the tools to make the right decisions—and everyone understands the core values—they always do the right thing; honestly, they will meet the challenge and exceed it."

Other changes started to percolate after the high-handed VP was let go. One example was a contract administrator who was going on her seventh or eighth year with the company. Her attendance was horrible, her face was always down, and her attitude was miserable. She was on the edge of getting fired and had a couple of write-ups for insubordination in her file. "I remember once I asked her for a contract and she kept eating her breakfast burrito with an, 'I'll get to it when I get to it' look on her face," says Shandon. But the newly minted CEO wasn't willing to give up on the long-term employee so fast—she understood the stress of working under the old VP and wanted to see whether she could bring her out of her shell. Besides, she saw that the Greatest Race had changed her attitude—a spark was ignited that hadn't been there before.

"We saw that enthusiasm and asked her if there was anything about the contracts process that she would change," says Shandon. "At first she resisted; she didn't believe us. But we said, 'You see things we just don't see.' Then, after the Amazing Race, she felt comfortable calling out some of the problems—and she was right about them. She has great ideas that were hidden under a layer of fear."

The employee also recently stopped a client from canceling an account, Shandon says with a great measure of pride. "This was a person who was on the line, and we said to her, 'We care about your input.' Now she is a different person, and in a few months, she was named Employee of the Year. This is a woman who cares for her disabled mom and an unemployed husband and teenage daughter. She used to bark at her daughter, but now she goes home proud and feels good about herself."

Shandon also welcomed people from other industries. "I have an EVP who has a background in computer and IT," she says. "Industry people aren't always the best problem solvers; often they have been trained by a big security firm, and they tend to be stuck there." One of the ways SDA competes is by doing things differently and more personally than its larger competitors, such as ADT. "We deal with a very high level of law enforcement, so we need innovators; people from outside the business often bring a fresh perspective."

Finally, Shandon writes employees an email once a week called "A View from the Harbour." "The managers talk about what we did that week," she explains. "It gives names to people who did a great job, whether it was bringing in a huge order, or the fact that we ran a call center successfully during a blackout. Whatever we accomplished that week goes into the letter. It's a chance for them to really be part of it."

When SDA recruits people from much larger companies, they often tell Shandon it's less about paycheck—they want to have a say and they want to work somewhere where they can believe in the culture and the mission. "Our fly wheel is going and it's about to take off."

INVESTING IN PEOPLE

Jonathan Citrin is the founder and CEO of CitrinGroup, an investment advisory firm in Birmingham, Michigan. "I met with Jonathan a few times prior to my start at CitrinGroup, and right away I could sense his kindness, which of course made me extremely excited to start working for him," says Carla Kouchary. Kindness isn't exactly the first thing you think of when you imagine an investment professional—it's a high-stress pressure-cooker world that doesn't always engender benevolence. "Jonathan doesn't approach his employees with power or fear, but as an equal player on the team. He understands that everyone has an important role and that maintaining high company morale is key," says Carla.

So how does he do it? Employees say Jonathan creates a comfortable atmosphere where they can be open with ideas and concerns because they know they won't go unanswered or unvalued. He's got "contagious excitement," says one, and his positive outlook is one of the prime reasons for the firm's continuous success.

"I started in investment several years ago, and when in 2000 the market crashed, a lot of people did not like it, but I had a great boss who made that time very interesting," says Jonathan. He started his own firm in 2003 after managing portfolios at Morgan Stanley. Before getting into the financial world, he had trained as an educator and taught school for several years—which is perhaps where his natural enthusiasm for showing the ropes to new employees comes from, at least in part.

> "We have a value statement not for marketing purposes, but that means something for employees, and that is 'the courage not to conform.'"
>
> —Jonathan Citrin

"I definitely brought my ideology from the classroom and my entrepreneurial streak to my own company," Jonathan says. "There's a book called *The First Days of School* that everyone reads when becoming a teacher. It's about setting the tone for the entire year in the first few days of classes. The author's approach is somewhat rigid. The idea is you have to be mean, and if you're not, you're screwed. Well, I decided to take a totally different approach. I was firm and respectful and led that way. I've taken that ideology to my business, and I have found it's what wonderful people—those who you want on your team—respond to."

The firm didn't run well overnight. "I did make some hiring mistakes in the beginning," Jonathan says. "It took a while for me to get better and to find people whose ideology fit with mine. I wanted to build a team of people who believed a financial company should be transparent and should stand for something more than just profits. We want to leave a positive mark on the world." People who just went through the motions or focused only on making money to the detriment of the company's reputation or customer service were let go. "Getting a strong team of like-minded individuals who also know how to disagree enabled me to be a CEO who didn't have to be at arm's length, strict, or manipulative. It is so much easier that way."

As a result, CitrinGroup has a close-knit team that works together without an exacting hierarchy. "It's a balancing act—accessibility is a lot about trust and giving people autonomy," says Jonathan. "I handle the framework of the business and allow my team to do what it does best—manage portfolios." In fact, he has a built-in BS meter in the form of a fellow Jonathan calls "The Blocker." "His role is to tell me how I am wrong and criticize me, and to make sure I'm not complimenting myself," Jonathan explains. "It takes someone with confidence to let go and take suggestions from employees."

The other strategy Jonathan uses to stay connected and accessible to his team is the way he holds meetings. "Our agendas are generative. Every internal meeting has at least one item on it that asks the team to stop and think outside the norm. We have a lot of intellectual capital at the firm, and I want to use every inch of it," he says. Meetings are also a time for everyone to be honest and tell each other what they think. "The slippery slope is that with such a focus, it would be so easy for me to force people to invest in one thing or another, and I could push people into a certain way of thinking. I have made a lot of good decisions, but I would have made not-so-good ones had I not built a team of trusted, smart people. I often just shut my mouth and count to ten if I think I know the answer and let someone else come up with an answer that's better than mine."

Aside from not bothering with meetings unless they have a creative or strategic purpose, Jonathan also gives employees time to step back from their jobs so they don't get caught up in the day-to-day. He encourages them to get outside, take walks, and participate in community activities.

There's one more thing that has improved the interconnectivity of the office—and that's a new, tighter focus at the firm. "Our team has become closer and our revenue has grown as we have focused the business on portfolio management instead of trying to be a full-service financial firm—we don't do taxes or sell insurance, for example," he says. This has not only mitigated risk but also enabled the team to concentrate on getting stellar performance from portfolios. "We manage $60 million of investor assets, which is down from a much larger number, because we could all be happier and more connected with a smaller and stronger business model. We run two portfolios, growth and income, and we strive to be great at it. The work is so much more meaningful—and exciting—than it was before."

Finally, Jonathan admits that he's as "OCD as the next guy," but being an asshole "is just too stressful. I learned through business how to let go and lead by example and let others do their thing." The benefits aren't only to the bottom line. "It's made me a much healthier person, and that's not just perception. My lower cholesterol, lower blood pressure numbers, and my healthy weight are testaments to the fact that being a nice, accessible boss has huge advantages. The more I let go, and the more I include the team in my business, the better I feel."

A PLACE AT THE TABLE

Joel Bomgar founded Bomgar Corporation, a tech-support company, in 2003, right after he graduated from college, and has made being nice a key component of his corporate culture. His college friend and co-founder is still with the company as chief strategy officer. A whopping 54 percent of the employees hired within Bomgar's first two years are still with the organization. Since he began the company, Joel has always been open and honest with all of his employees, treating them as equals rather than as direct reports. He encourages them to work remotely if need be and to strike the right balance between personal and professional life. Bomgar is also extremely family friendly, with each employee receiving not only paternity/maternity leave but also $500 should he or she have a baby; the company offers $10,000 in adoption assistance as well.

"One of the things we have observed about workers is that their willingness to stay loyal has gone down in the last generation," says Joel. "However, we find it easy to recruit because we can find people from companies who felt they were not treated well or they were working for people with an old mentality." Bomgar employees feel privileged to work at the company, and there's a real sense that they're working for a team that is changing the world. "The millennial generation is loyal to companies that are loyal to them," says Joel. "If they don't like their boss, they will get another job. They just don't put up with stuff our parents put up with. So there's a real penalty for people who aren't nice." Employees can post or check out companies on places like Glass Door and find out how people are treated even before they apply for a job. And they do. It's the same with customer service—people can very easily check how you treat customers before they do business with you. "It's a transparent world out there, so you really don't have a choice. You have to be nice," says Joel, who has made it his business to be benevolent and transparent—literally.

> "Everyone is on the same page here, sharing the same information, top to bottom. I never understood executives who think employees aren't smart enough to digest company information."
>
> —Joel Bomgar

"I have a deep belief in the true equality of people, and so I value the work that every staff member does at Bomgar," says Joel. "That was the premise I based the company on, and from that point of view, transparency springs naturally. If you value your contributors, you want them to know what's going on." Joel and his management team provide regular company updates, and they make an effort to be very public on deals that close and those that don't. "A typical employee in another company would not know this information, but we make it known so that everyone feels like they are part of the team. If all you're telling people is to work hard and trust us, the quality of work you're after is not going to get to the level you want to achieve," argues Joel.

Perhaps the most innovative way Joel stays connected to his staff is through Tuesday Lunch. "I try to sit at a different table every week, and I use that time to see how things are going on the front lines. I get a real sense of what's important and what's not important to employees. It's really a great way to get rid of barriers," he says. It gives Joel a chance to explain things that don't make sense or to answer questions—or just talk about whatever is going on, inside or outside the office. Lunch provides a relaxed atmosphere. The entire management team also attends Tuesday lunch. It's easy to schedule over it, but the company and Joel really emphasize the importance of Tuesdays to the entire leadership team. "To make it more fun, employees can request certain food—pizza, pasta, sandwiches, and if revenues are good, we can do something fancy," he says.

On the first Tuesday of every month, Joel also gets up in front of the group, or dials in from wherever he is if he's out of town, and tells people about the deals they've made, which ones they lost out on, how much money they have in the bank, and what the company's high-level strategies are. It's a level of transparency that most companies don't come close to reaching. "A person from each department of the company also goes over highlights from the management meeting. There is a lot more communication that the entire employee base is getting. We also make sure the employees we have in other locations (ten states and three different countries) are dialed in to participate," he says.

"At the First Tuesday update I also cover our core values," he continues. A lot of those values address the fundamentals and how employee relationships should develop—through mutual respect, exchange of ideas, and healthy disagreement. In 2010, Joel started another feedback program called Leadership 360. "It's a survey that lists the name of every person in leadership. Employees rate on two things: how effective they are in their job function and how effective they are in instilling and living out our core values. And I let the entire employee base provide that feedback. Overall, we did pretty well. It creates an environment where there is a clear expectation of how leaders should behave. They should have understood the culture. We don't promote people unless they are being nice and playing fair—it's critical to what we do."

Bomgar also has a company-wide bonus plan that is stunning in its equality and balance. Every quarter, employees can earn a certain amount of bonus money. If the company achieves 50 percent of the goal that was set, everyone shares that 50 percent. Joel's personal bonus is tied to the same number, and employees know it. The bonus targets are generally achievable and are set by the board of directors. "I get the same percentage as employees do. We are in the same boat. If we miss a bonus, I don't get a single penny. You get an incredible alignment from that," says Joel. "No one gets an unfair benefit, no matter how the company is doing."

Have all these strategies worked for the company? Yes. "We have actually been able to keep up with double-digit growth," says Joel. "In 2009 we did 14 percent, and we did 33 percent growth from last year in 2010. The reality is it is tough out there, and we are doing better than a lot of companies, and it's all the more important to be in the boat with employees."

SUMMARY OF KEY POINTS

Accessible leaders

- Engender an attitude of mutual respect and kindness;
- Make sure there are connections between junior and senior people on an ongoing basis;
- Are sensibly available to all constituents;
- Convey an attitude of approachability;
- Ensure that everyone understands core values, mission, and expectations;
- Play fair with information, bonuses, expectations, and workloads;
- Walk the shop (or office) floor and are visible;
- Don't hide in an ivory tower, talk openly;
- Know when to keep their mouths shut and let others do the talking;
- Communicate simply, honestly, and in plain English—on a consistent basis, whether it's daily, weekly, or monthly—in a verbal or written format; and

- Build a culture of collaboration as part of the management strategy. Learning together (across ranks) helps people work better together.

5

TRAIT #3

Strategic Listening

"I only wish I could find an institute that teaches people how to listen. Business people need to listen at least as much as they need to talk. Too many people fail to realize that real communication goes in both directions."

—Lee Iacocca, former CEO, Chrysler Corporation

Nature gave us two ears and one mouth, clearly indicating that it's more important to listen than to talk. I pity the person most who sits next to me on an airplane, because I like to connect with people and hear their story. That's how I met a Miss Texas on one flight and countless other people I now count as clients or colleagues or even friends on other flights. Listening is the most beneficial thing we can do that uses the least amount of physical energy. Aside from the entertaining aspect of growing a conversation (not just waiting for a break in it so you can steer the conversation toward you), it's an incredibly valuable and profitable tool.

I've met strangers in airports who have gone on to become clients not because I spent time promoting myself to them but because I got them to open up by asking questions and absorbing their answers. People love to be heard and understood. We crave it—by listening, you're fulfilling a primal need of another person; if they happen to be customers, you're doing so much more than just selling something. To listen well is a powerful tool, not only for learning and understanding, but for creating influence as well—I'm determined to convince you of this because I fully recognize that "be a good listener" is advice everyone gives but no one takes seriously, right up there with "work out" and "drink more water."

Why? For one thing, listening is damn hard work. On a practical level, I understand that we are completely wrapped up in the demands of obligation. If you're trying to build something, to get ahead, you've got responsibilities. There's a lot on your plate, what with managing fiscal responsibilities, operations, meetings, production, and so on. Distractions are endless—and enticing. Technology makes them accessible—how many times did you check your smartphone during a meeting? Mmm . . . Twitter . . . Ooh!! Shiny! How many times has someone said something you didn't remember a word of simply because you were thinking of something else? Listening is also challenging because it requires us to consider people we don't even know or like.

One of the problems is that listening is low on the priority list for leadership. In the management research world, listening is considered a "soft skill," along with being a team player, accepting criticism, and flexibility. Steven Neil Kaplan, professor of entrepreneurship and finance at the University of Chicago Booth School of Business, and his colleagues did a study called "Which CEO Characteristics and Abilities Matter?" The study, published in the June 2012 issue of the *Journal of Finance,* looked at the individual characteristics of CEO candidates for companies involved in buyout and venture capital transactions and compared these characteristics to subsequent corporate performance. It concluded that good listening skills didn't make a whit of difference to the success of those leaders. Anyone reading the authors' results would come away with the idea that honing listening skills is a complete waste of time. Why bother to get better at it? If the experts say it's got little to do with running a profitable business, what the hell, give me the cotton—I've got ears to plug.

Except that not everyone, including me, agrees that listening is a soft skill. Meet Dr. Richard D. Halley, emeritus professor of communication at Weber State University and the lead facilitator of the Certified Listening Professional Program (Lee Iacocca would be thrilled to know that there is actually an institution that helps people learn to listen). "Listening is not a soft skill, it is hard to do," says Halley. "It takes a long time to learn to listen well, because it takes knowledge and perspective to listen well, and that does not come without effort. Good listeners spend more energy than nonlisteners; they burn more calories and feel tired after listening well to another person or people." I can attest to that.

The reason that some people, especially those in management, categorize listening as a soft skill is the perspective they take when thinking about a communication event, according to Halley. "They tend to think of it in an interpersonal context, and that's why there's a tendency to say women are better listeners than men, which is just not true. Many perspectives on listening are flawed in this regard; women's brains are wired to attend to emotional data, so it is easier for them to pay attention to what's being said in a relationship. Change the task to one that is not focused on personal relationships and on something a male is more interested in, and he becomes a much better listener. Research shows that among people who take a comprehension test after listening to a lecture, guys always do better." Halley contends that if you asked hedge fund managers or CEOs how they obtained the information they use to make their organizations work well, they would have to admit it was through listening to things they were interested in and that were tied to the needs of their business.

Another important point Halley makes about effective listeners is that they—not the guy flapping his gums—are the ones who control the interaction. Sure, the speaker can shut his mouth anytime he wants. But the guy who's standing in front of him may have stopped listening a long time ago, thereby intentionally and unintentionally ending the interaction. We have a bias toward speaking in this culture, but if you choose not to listen, the speaker is cut off. That's a double-edged sword, of course, because if you do stop listening, you could be cut off.

If you're not out there engaging clients, customers, and employees, you're going to miss a lot, including danger signals that relate to both your personal position and your company's position within the marketplace. Consider Brian Dunn, who stepped down as CEO of Best Buy in May 2012—just three years after being given the top job—for having an inappropriate relationship with a younger female subordinate. That was the main reason he had to go, but the fact that the electronic retailer also announced a $1.7 billion quarterly loss along with big layoffs and the closure of 50 of its 100 stores shortly before the scandal broke probably didn't help Dunn's position much either.

In 2009 *Fortune* magazine reporter Marc Gunther interviewed Dunn shortly after he took the corner office at Best Buy (he'd been an employee for more than a quarter of a century) and asked how he stayed connected to staff and customers. "One of my roles as CEO is to be the chief listener," Dunn said. "I don't believe that the model is that there are a few really smart people at the top of the pyramid that make all the strategic decisions. It is much more about being an all-around enterprise and looking for people with great ideas and passionate points of view that are anchored to the business and connected to things our customers care about."

Something obviously happened to Dunn's "listening ears" between the time *Fortune* called and the time Best Buy's board asked him to leave. If he had continued to take his own advice, he would have known and acted on what the board found out during its probe of and report on the situation—that "a growing awareness and speculation surrounding the friendship created friction and disruption in the workplace and, according to her supervisor, impeded efforts to supervise" the subordinate.

It's crucial to hear danger signals, which are often weak and hidden because we don't like bad news. In particular, people tend to hide bad news from the boss. You also have to really trust the people around you to give you the right information—and if they believe you do listen to them without constantly criticizing or one-upping them, honesty will be easier to come by.

Eventually, executives who don't listen lose the support of their board, colleagues, employees, and customers, Brian Dunn being case in point. Surely he knew his relationship was common knowledge—he left an easily followed trail of workplace evidence of the liaison behind him. The board found dozens of emails, text messages, and phone calls between the two carried out during business hours and on company equipment.

Poor listening skills not only eat away at relationships, they also have a negative effect on decision making, implementation, and innovation. If you aren't listening to the marketplace, how can you sense change or fulfill needs? How do you know your customers are happy? Of course, in Best Buy's case, a variety of consumer and economic forces contributed to its financial losses. Could those losses have been prevented if Dunn had been paying attention to what was happening in the marketplace? Was he listening to his team members about issues at the store level? Was he giving manufacturers a chance to weigh in on what was going on in the industry? Or was he arrogant enough to believe these things didn't matter?

Jon Corzine, the former governor of New Jersey, was ousted as head of Goldman Sachs in 1999, and a decade later he found himself at the center of the $40 billion implosion of his brokerage firm, MF Global, complete with $1.2 billion in missing client funds. I don't know what's worse—Corzine's claim that he didn't know anything about what happened to the money in what is a small company, or that he did know and ignored what was going on. Either way, it adds up to a bad listener. As *Vanity Fair's* Bryan Burrough, William D. Cohan, and Bethany McLean reported in February 2012, "As a CEO, he was far more at ease issuing orders than listening. 'That was always Jon's biggest problem,' recalls a Goldman colleague. 'I remember our chairman, John Weinberg, telling me once that it was Jon's biggest flaw: that he didn't listen.'"

Rubbermaid CEO Wolfgang Schmitt was famous for showing off his ability to sort out difficult issues on the fly. One former colleague remembers that people would joke that "Wolf knows everything about everything." In one discussion, the employee recalls, a group was reviewing a complicated acquisition the company had made in Europe, and Wolf, without hearing different points of view, announced, "This is what we are going to do." The problem with leaders who feel they have all the answers is, well, what if they're wrong? Wolf, unfortunately, was wrong. Under his know-it-all leadership, Rubbermaid went from being *Fortune's* most admired company in America in 1993 to being acquired by a conglomerate, Newell, a few years later.

Biotech giant Amgen's CEO Kevin Sharer was, for a long time, guilty of dismissing or ignoring what others had to say. He told consultant McKinsey & Company, "For most of my career, I was an awful listener in almost every possible way. I was arrogant throughout my 30s for sure—maybe into my early 40s. My conversations were all about some concept of intellectual winning and 'I'm going to prove I'm smarter than you.' It wasn't an evil, megalomania-driven thing; it was mostly because I was a striver, I wanted to get ahead, and getting ahead meant convincing people of my point of view." This view is shared by many of us, especially as we climb the ladder. When we "make it," we may have gotten so used to competing and persuading by talking and doing that we fail to realize that we have to prove ourselves in a different way—by shutting up and paying attention and then basing strategy on what we've learned.

Sharer got lucky—he had a moment of self-revelation and insight when surprise, surprise, he *listened* to a talk by Sam Palmisano, president and CEO of IBM from 2002 to 2011. Palmisano was asked why his experience working in Japan was so important to his leadership development. "I learned to listen by having only one objective: comprehension. I was only trying to understand what the person was trying to convey to me. I wasn't listening to critique or object or convince," he said.

That was an epiphany for Sharer: "Because as you become a senior leader, it's a lot less about convincing people and more about benefiting from complex information and getting the best out of the people you work with," he says. "Listening for comprehension helps you get that information, of course, but it's more than that: it's also the greatest sign of respect you can give someone."

Sharer's method of listening is engaging people in the company who don't necessarily report to him as well as reading as much as possible, including employee and customer surveys, operating data, analyst reports, regulatory reports, and outside analyses. Sharer meets with Amgen's top-ten investors twice a year to listen, and at shareholder conferences he considers the Q & A session essential to growing the business. "The key is making yourself open to the possibility that information can and will come from almost anywhere," he says. The next step is acting on what you learn, which is why he calls listening a "threshold skill." If you don't have it, you will fail. But having it doesn't guarantee success if you don't act appropriately on what you're hearing or if you're no good at analyzing what's being said and figuring out what it means. This is called strategic listening.

Want to try something similar to train your brain to listen for comprehension only? I do this all the time: try proofreading something you've just written—an email, a memo, whatever, by reading it backward, from the last word to the first. When you do it this way, you're training your brain to look for errors, to *comprehend*, not to attack or dismantle.

When A. G. Lafley stepped down as CEO of Procter & Gamble in 2009, he received across-the-board accolades for his management and marketing abilities—everyone from competitors to business journalists sang his praises. During his eight-year tenure at the helm of P&G (he started out at the company in 1977 as a brand assistant for Joy liquid detergent), corporate culture went from being buttoned up, top down, and insular to open, collaborative, and innovative. Do you use Febreze? So do I. Thank Lafley. Revenues doubled under his watch, thanks in part to incredible product development that answered the needs of consumers.

Aside from his strategic acumen and a strong belief in the transformative power of marketing and design, Lafley had a commitment to listening, particularly to consumer needs and behaviors, and to employee ideas. "The consumer is boss" was his company mantra. He followed his own advice and, in fact, was quite famous for traveling the world to talk with actual consumers. He met them in their homes to find out what products they used, how they used them, and why. There was nothing more fascinating to him than watching a woman in Spain or New York play around with her collection of hair products. Trips to the grocery store with customers helped him understand how people make buying decisions. Observation is another form of listening. What he and his team members learned from these expeditions would often become the seeds of successful and solution-oriented products. When you actually watch what people do in your company or with your product or service, you learn a great deal about what they want. These unspoken messages provide great insight into what's really going on.

If you're not used to listening—and it does take some practice—the following case studies will be enlightening. They demonstrate how 360-degree feedback makes an important difference
in how entrepreneurs grow successful businesses. Consciousness,
catching yourself before you zone out, is something you have to
develop as a habit, like working out or brushing your teeth. Leaders who listen strategically tend to:

1. Open yourself to chance encounters. My whole life seems
   to be a series of chance encounters, and I actually seek
   them out or put myself in a position to have them. I've
   met a lot of really interesting people and learned a lot
   from them about my business as well as businesses that
   could use my skills.
2. Have outer-directed awareness. Sharer says he learned to
   listen for "comprehension," but that won't happen unless
   you are tuned in to the speaker, whether it's one person or
   a group of consumers.
3. Show intention. The quality of listening is governed by
   the intention behind it. Sharer focused his listening on
   understanding what the other person was trying to say.
   This was a conscious decision on his part, and that's what
   enabled him to change his habit.
4. Suspend judgment. Hold back criticisms or sharing your
   opinion of what's being said until you've had a chance
   to reflect on it. This doesn't mean nodding your head
   in senseless agreement—it just means giving what you
   learned some thought before reaching a conclusion.
5. Ask open-ended questions. Give people a chance to
   expand on what they're saying, which allows them to
   learn more about their own feelings, which deepens your
   understanding and leads to the truth about a situation.

6. If nothing else—for Pete's sake, just have fun. Live life with a desire to enjoy what you're doing as much as possible, and you'll find people drawn to you, wanting to talk. All you have to do then is listen.

LISTENING IS IN THEIR DNA

Nazim Ahmed is co-founder of CanvasPop.com, an Internet retail company that is one of the fastest growing photo-to-canvas printing companies in North America. Mashable, *Forbes, Entrepreneur,* and the *Wall Street Journal,* among other media outlets, have covered the company and its two young founders, Ahmed and Adrian Salamunovic. Ahmed has launched several programs to encourage information gathering for the purposes of improving customer service and the employee experience. These constant "listening" improvements, including the development of products that differentiate them in a crowded marketplace, have paid off significantly.

Since CanvasPop creates custom artwork with a customer's own art—whatever that might mean—customer experience is critical for its growth, particularly because of the importance of social media and empowered customers' ability to voice cheers and jeers. Before CanvasPop, Ahmed started DNA11 with his best friend. "We each took a sample of our DNA sequencing and turned the results into abstract art. That was in 2005, without a notion that it would be a business," says Ahmed. But after *CSI* used a piece of the DNA art as an integral part of one of its story lines, the business went crazy. "We wanted to keep making the experience better for customers, because at that point every sale was critical for our survival. When we decided to do it full-time, we spoke to every single customer, took orders personally, and built a relationship. That was our obsession, a strong customer experience, and we embedded what we learned from them into everything we did," he says. Customers responded—amazing things happen when people feel someone is listening to them.

One customer request often heard was the desire to get artwork sooner. So the company brought printing production in-house because outsourcing was causing delays. By 2009 everything had been brought in-house, from the entire printing and shipping facility to the DNA lab itself. Ahmed has a degree in genetics and worked for a biotech company before starting the DNA art company, developing imaging systems and robotics. His partner is a web marketing and design person, so the match seemed perfect. At first, none of the labs Ahmed approached wanted to take on the business, but eventually he found one company that thought the idea was crazy and interesting enough to take a shot at it, in part because the owner was an art enthusiast. Now, because of the success of the company, it has a biotech lab right in the middle of the factory.

When customers started asking for other images to be printed on canvas, the duo thought it was another viable business. "We had become experts on DNA digital printing, so we thought, why not offer the service of putting any cool photo on a quality canvas," says Ahmed. That's an example of listening—what started as a one-off service for loyal customers and friends became part of the company's infrastructure and was soon leveraged into an entirely new company, CanvasPop.

> "We feel customers are our friends, and we talk to them like friends. What you hear is amazing."
>
> —Nazim Ahmed

Listening also enabled the team to make some smart organizational decisions. It went to Las Vegas after listening to various people in the industry who told them that amazing printing professionals who wanted to work but had lost jobs because of what had happened to the hospitality industry after the 2008 recession were available. Finding good printing people on the West Coast of the United States also enabled CanvasPop to deliver all across North America faster.

Since orders are placed through reps online and on the phone (obviously the founders can no longer personally take every order), employees had to be empowered to make the right decisions for the customer without going through a lot of management layers. They had to be able to make the right decisions on the spot, decisions that were also in keeping with the company's customer service ethos. "That cost us money in the beginning, because we would solve any problem that cropped up, any dissatisfaction with any aspect of the product was taken care of immediately, no questions asked," says Ahmed. Because a redo is expensive in the canvas printing business, it was expensive for CanvasPop in the short term to respond to complaints—even if mistakes were customer errors (i.e., the measurements they provided for the final product were inaccurate and distorted the reproduced image in a negative or unexpected fashion).

"If it was a problem, the service person could have a genuine conversation with the customer and act appropriately in terms of what the customer was telling them, instead of stiffly following a script," says Ahmed. This way, not only did they build valuable trusted relationships and repeat business, but they actually heard a lot of interesting things from customers that helped them build the business—something that never would have happened had service reps worked with scripts they could not veer from. There's nothing more annoying than listening to what you think might be an actual person sound like a robot without a mind of its own. "We feel customers are our friends, and we talk to them like friends. What you hear is amazing," says Ahmed.

What they heard was often gleaned from blogs and social media postings from happy customers. Some of the changes the company has instituted from listening are longer customer service hours (Ahmed notes, "No matter how small you are, customers are used to and expect 24/7, so you have to push to get there. I add hours and days to support regularly, and eventually we will get to 24/7"), short-turnaround Christmas and holiday shipping, and faster overall turnaround and delivery times without compromising quality.

CanvasPop guarantees its products for life because of the fairly expensive procedure they use to laminate and heat seal the images on the canvas material. The process protects the image and surface from fading and scratching. "We know we have to deliver a great product, we heard that from customers," Ahmed says. "We don't compete on price, we are not in a race to the bottom. If you focus on driving to the bottom, you will go to a bad place, and that's not differentiating yourself in a good way. We compete on the promise of quality and service, like many great products—Apple, for example, doesn't sell the cheapest phones or laptops on the market, but you can argue they sell the best service and quality."

In order to make listening effective, Ahmed uses what he calls "root cause analysis" to look at every problem, identify its source, and then immediately implement and institutionalize the solution so the issue never or rarely comes up again. "Our goal eventually is that our customer gets the highest quality product in the shortest time and that it's a cohesive experience that does not even necessitate a call to customer service, ever, except to say hello, great job," he says. Until they reach that point, Ahmed plans to continue to keep customers happy by resolving any problem immediately and to continue to develop strong relationships between reps and managers so that the root cause of the problem can be pinpointed and corrected quickly.

As a testament to the power of listening, both companies have been profitable since they started. Conversations on social media make it clear the company is sticking by its mantra of listening and responding to customers and employees. "Go on Twitter and you see long conversations about how great CanvasPop is. You see comments like, here's my canvas, they are the best, so go with them," says Ahmed. "We held back from entering those conversations; they happen naturally because every person on the floor is obsessed with the same thing I am, quality. We talk about it every quarter with managers, and managers talk to everyone on the floor about it every day. The guys who stretch canvases are thinking about how to make each canvas perfect—when they find a way, we listen and act."

A GOLD STAR FOR PAYING ATTENTION

Daniel Milstein, 34, is CEO of Gold Star Mortgage Financial Group in Ann Arbor, Michigan. The company has revenues of about $19 million and employs 400 people. *Inc.* magazine named Gold Star one of its 500 Fastest Growing Companies. After emigrating from the former Soviet Union to metropolitan Detroit when he was 16 years old, Milstein worked after school to help his family make ends meet. "I had 17 cents in my pocket when I arrived, and I was fortunate to get a job as a bank teller with TCF Bank [at age 19]," says Milstein. After stints with Comerica Bank and CitiMortgage, Milstein founded Gold Star in 2000.

Gold Star was listed No. 349 on the *Inc.* 500 list, recording 712.8 percent revenue growth from 2005 to 2008. "We provide home financing [for everyone from] first-time homebuyers to celebrities," Milstein says. "When the global financial meltdown hit, I knew we could get through it. I'm confident I could sell sand in the desert, but [at the time] we cleaned out our balance sheet and put the pedal to the metal. We never engaged in subprime lending, which got a lot of financial companies in trouble. We also quadrupled our advertising and marketing, which proved to be a big help."

Gold Star has an extremely low turnover rate for the industry, and Milstein says it's because he treats employees like family. "I know their professional lives and personal lives, and my door is always open for them to come in and discuss issues, failures, and successes," he says. The company never pushed employees to write bad loans, which came back to bite so many other mortgage companies, Milstein says, because he listened to the market and to employees. He never wanted to create an atmosphere that pressured sales people to do things that would ultimately have a negative impact on the business. Maybe they didn't write as many mortgages as other companies—but where did that get other companies in the long run?

Listening helped Milstein move up the ladder too—an important lesson for would-be CEOs. He worked his way up from assistant consumer lending manager, general manager, and underwriter to become chief operations officer within various financial institutions. "Mainly I learned by observing and listening carefully to others—and acting on what I saw and heard. I learned what to do and what not to do by working with and watching managers I had throughout my life. I always make sure to show my employees that, as the leader, I am the first one in each day and the last one out. I am always available for them, nights, weekends, because I want to know what they're seeing in the market and how they're feeling about the work. It's invaluable in making the right decisions in this business," he says.

> "Knock on my door, let me know what's happening right now. It's the only way you can find out market conditions and strategize for the future climates."
> —Daniel Milstein

In 1999, Milstein was an underwriter in another firm, and he started seeing pay stubs and W-2 forms from the employees of the big three carmakers. At the same time, he saw car prices doubling year after year. He knew that the phenomenon of highly paid line workers and expensive car prices couldn't be sustained for long (and he was right). "Those line guys were buying $500–600K homes without a high school education, and at the time you were not encouraged to say no in lending," he says. "It did not make sense to me not to do a verification of employment when you were about to give someone a half-a-million-dollar loan without down payment money. At that point in time we were looking at markets, and we decided not to get into subprime lending because of what I saw. We were flying under the radar because we were smaller at the time, and our credit guidelines assured us we could find mortgage clients with verifiable credit and income. It was just a matter of time before the bottom would fall out."

When he started Gold Star, Milstein stuck to the principle of listening to the market and making decisions based on what he heard. While other mortgage companies went under, Gold Star thrived. "My biggest competitors in the local market became my employees because they were forced to close their doors—60 percent of the local mortgage companies went under," Milstein says. "That worked out well for us, because we retained highly experienced people whose companies underestimated the market and jumped on subprime. I say to them, do not look at clients for their ability to make money—do the best you can and the money will follow."

The other lesson Milstein learned is that the mortgage business is largely a referral-based business. "What I found out is if you do a loan with someone who has bad credit, they don't refer their friends and family to you. Referrals based on good customers are the best." It's a policy he has taught his team.

"I am always on the go, I do not have time to meet with employees in formal scheduled meetings. That's why I always make myself available, so people are encouraged to talk to me about a deal when it's happening. I don't want people to hold back their feelings. Knock on my door, let me know what's happening right now. It's the only way you can find out market conditions and strategize for the future climates. Waiting to learn that information in a meeting scheduled two weeks from now is useless, it's too late," says Milstein.

Milstein also keeps his ear to the ground by personally hand-delivering everyone's mail once a month and handing out cookies. That way he can talk to employees in a relaxed fashion and find out what they're working on without the pressure of a weekly meeting. "I run the only company, I assure you, where all executives must sell loans. They have to do these transactions because I want them to know what it is like to clear a loan. There are managers in this business who have not sold a loan in 20 years—how can they relate to the person selling loans on a regular basis unless they've done it themselves recently? They can't really listen to these people in a relevant fashion unless they know exactly what they're up against. You can't do that if the last time you filled out paperwork was two decades ago," Milstein points out.

Unfortunately, Milstein notes that many people don't necessarily learn from experience—in other words, they never listen. "While the mortgage crisis will never get to the level we saw in 2008, no doubt subprime loans will make a comeback. I am already seeing signs of it happening again. People have a short memory; just because you're having a good month doesn't mean the subprime business is going to be any different than it ever was," he says.

HOW MANY LISTENERS DOES IT TAKE TO CHANGE A LIGHT BULB?

Joe Scaretta co-founded Empire Facilities Management Group with his partner Moses Carrasco in 2003, when he was only 21 years old. Empire provides businesses a one-stop shop for a variety of services from painting to energy reduction to rebuilds. The business works across North America, serving more than 150 clients with a diverse nationwide network of over 30,000 subcontractors.

And to think it all started in a baseball cage. "We came from the trenches," says Scaretta. "I came from large retailers, and what bothered both Moses and I was that we'd hear great information at the store level, and we knew how to compete from a corporate standpoint, but upper management didn't listen." That might be because, basically, Scaretta was a teenager when he tried giving advice to executives who may have been twice his age or more. It's tough to listen to a kid who could be your son about how to run your business better. But maybe they should have listened anyway.

"When working for my first nationwide retail sporting store, I had the keys to its five largest stores in the country," Scaretta remembers. "They moved me to another store in the chain that was underperforming and losing money badly. We put processes in place to right the ship and improve customer experience and profitability. I came up with a top-down marketing campaign and promotion called Baseball Day. At that time, the marketing was done corporate to store, not store to corporate." Somehow, Scaretta talked the regional rep into letting him run the program. That rep gave the kid a chance—easier said than done. Scaretta got Paul Gibson's All Pro Sports Academy to place one of its 50-foot batting cages in the store, along with a couple of instructors, including former New York Yankee and New York Mets pitcher Paul Gibson.

One of the oddities of most sporting goods stores is that they traditionally do not allow customers to try out bats before making a purchase decision. You had to buy a bat and take it home to try, according to Scaretta. During Baseball Day, however, kids could wear their team's uniform, try out a bat in the cage, and save 10 percent if they (or their parents) decided to buy. "Based on this marketing event, the store made in excess of $40,000 over the planned revenue for the weekend," Scaretta says. He was an energetic guy, so Paul Gibson's Sports Camps courted Scaretta to take on a marketing and public relations role, but something was missing. "I did it for a short period of time, but eventually I moved into facility management. I worked for a small, successful company, but it was frustrating. The owner was set in his ways and didn't listen to the people in the trenches who were talking to the end user every day. A lot of executives don't get that," he says. One good thing came out of the experience—Scaretta met his future partner, and the two of them thought they could do facility management better.

They opened Empire as a traditional facility management company—doing maintenance and repairs for retailers nationwide. But what they heard and saw from clients was a need for services that weren't normally being offered by facility management firms. Basically, a retail or professional establishment historically had two choices: either maintain existing assets or undertake complete remodels. There weren't many facility managers offering hybrid services that meshed maintenance with simple renovation services.

"Today we run nationwide support throughout the country and can deal with almost any request—from fixing or replacing flooring, lighting, ceiling tiles, general maintenance, plumbing, carpentry, line striping, building, storage solutions, and landscaping," Scaretta says. The model works because Empire can dispatch prequalified vendors they keep on a database, and then the company verifies that the work was done, closes out the work order, and lets the client know the work has been completed. The focus on work that's too small for a normal general contractor but too large for a traditional handyman or repair services has filled a genuine need in the market.

"Our top ten or 20 clients want a fix and refresh: full flooring replacement, installation of millwork, painting and other tasks done after hours that can really refresh a store without going through a complete renovation," says Scaretta. The strategy of giving customers what they wanted helped the company through a tough economy. "People still have to maintain locations—when you go into a high-end retail store, even though the economy is down, the store has an obligation to maintain brand integrity."

> "We know from listening to clients that anything we can do to save them money gets us more work ultimately."
>
> —Joe Scaretta

Another core of the business is finding and implementing customer solutions. "We call it reducing costs without sacrificing brand image. That includes networking programmable thermostats and installing window film that cuts down on energy costs without having any negative impact on the space itself," says Scaretta. The partners identified the top-ten items for energy reduction and became the largest implementation company for these products. "Our clients can save on average an estimated 30–40 percent on their energy bills by having us come in and tailor an energy program that fits their needs. One manufacturer of programmable thermostats wanted to be our exclusive supplier, [but] we turned them down because we recognized that one of our successes as a company is we offer our clients multiple options to truly find the right product that fits their needs instead of being forced to buy one specific brand."

The other secret to Empire's success (Guess, Sprint, and Aéropostale have all named Empire "Vendor of the Year" more than once) is listening to what Scaretta calls clients' "pain points" and responding to them. This approach keeps the company competitive and nimble and builds client loyalty. Isn't it a relief when you find a company or a person who can just take care of the things that are your own pain points? Why would you go somewhere else if that need is being met beyond expectations?

For example, traditionally, you would have to paint at least an entire wall, if not all four of them, to accommodate a touch-up when refreshing paint. And the cost associated with a full-store painting or the frequency with which a full painting is needed is a pain point for clients. Empire has spent time sourcing and working to procure a paint product (currently under trial) that dramatically reduces both cost and frequency of full-store painting needs for their clients. "Most companies would shy away from offering this kind of solution because they fear losing bigger, more lucrative paint jobs. But we know from listening to clients that anything we can do to help reduce their cost and add value will help solidify our position as a trusted advisor," says Scaretta. Facility expenses come right from the bottom line—for every $1 saved on facility maintenance, $13 is saved in revenue, according to Scaretta's calculations. "Our long-term goal is to eventually take a company's facility department and give it positive cash flow."

Another pain point was the time it took to do a cosmetic remodel. "In the past, a client using a large general contractor for a cosmetic remodel had to shut down a store for five days or more," says Scaretta. "Moses and I studied the store, in this case a national accessories chain, to figure out why it took so long. We devised a model program that only required a two-and-a-half-day shutdown, which, for retail, is a huge timesaving. We are always looking for better ways to roll out capital projects, source out service calls, and bundle services for volume discounts."

Empire's customer retention rate is very high; Scaretta estimates that in more than nine years of business it has lost no more than two or three clients. And they do not hesitate to terminate clients when the partners don't agree with a client's business practices.

When a potential client asks Scaretta what benefit Empire can bring to the table, it's easy to answer the question. "We have accountability," he says. "We're nimble, dependable, and we're not afraid to the think outside the box. That's what clients want. [That's] what makes our National Vendor Database such a strong asset and allows our group to offer better pricing and services to the retailer, even if it may use the same vendor." They may call a vendor once a month. "We may call the same vendor 20 times a week and give him a lot of dependable work. That results in responsive vendors who do a good job at a great price because they want to keep getting our calls."

Empire also established a retail summit, which gathers together strategic vendors and clients so that everyone can share pain points and learn about their peers' best practices. "It's nice to spend time with peers who generally have similar issues and share solutions. As a vendor it helps us understand current trends and come up with new client services," says Scaretta. Seminars about trends in the industry, best practices, and cost-effective retailer-to-retailer solutions give participants a chance to learn what's working for other businesses in terms of facility management and maintenance. Scaretta sees only benefits from getting clients under one roof: "The way everybody looks at it is, if retail does well, everyone keeps their jobs."

Scaretta is also willing to solve problems that are generally not in their suite of services—why not? If one client needs something done, then there are probably others who want the same thing. "I met a client for a 2011 fiscal revenue of best practices, trends, and money saving strategies," he recounts. "The department manager was in the meeting, and she was stressed out trying to find a way to optimize space in a stock room. It was a sidebar conversation, and she revealed her frustration with a consulting firm that had charged a large fee for shelving ideas it couldn't implement—and the project had to be delivered to her VP. I asked to take a look, and I gave her four or five different solutions that would be low to no cost. What we can dream, we can build, because we have the right strategic partners and craftsmen who are able and willing." Empire created a PowerPoint presentation of the options, which the manager submitted to her VP. It was a huge pat on the back, because the solution they picked was more operationally sound and a far better price point. "I'd rather give away a couple of ideas to build a client relationship," says Scaretta. "We want a long-term relationship, and you can only get there by listening and executing."

SUMMARY OF KEY POINTS

Leaders who practice strategic listening

- Make sure they understand what someone is saying instead of simply taking in the words and forgetting them later;
- Act on what they see and hear in the marketplace— listening is useless without action; and
- Understand the deeper meaning of what clients say to get to the root of what they want—to paraphrase Henry Ford, if you ask people want they want, they'll tell you a faster horse. Know which words have the most meaning.

6

TRAIT #4

Good Stewardship

"I believe that every right implies a responsibility; every opportunity an obligation; every possession a duty."

—John D. Rockefeller Jr.

"Get it done."

—One of the mottos of the US Navy SEALs

It's no accident that good stewardship comes immediately after strategic listening. First, let me clarify what I mean by good stewardship. It's broader than having a concern for the environment—although it certainly includes that. It's also not just about leaving the world around you in a better state than you found it. Good stewardship is about responsible management and ethical standards that are in sync with the concerns of all the constituents who are important to your business, including shareholders, stakeholders, investors, neighbors, and communities. In order to be successful at it, you have to *listen for* and respond to social and political trends that can and will affect your company's standing in the public eye—and, as a result, its bottom line.

Interesting caveat here—you don't *have* to do this, and you might even get away with not doing it for a while. But this much is true: it will catch up to you, it will be hideous when it does, and it will remove all the short-term gains of not doing it. And then it will kick your ass on top of that.

Companies have a great deal of potential to be positive agents of change. As a leader, you're obligated to be involved in the social debates that can affect your industry. "At some point the media will find you and drag you into the conversation whether you like it or not," says Ronn Torossian, founder and CEO of one of the 25 largest PR firms, 5W Public Relations, and author of *For Immediate Release: Shape Minds, Build Brands, and Deliver Results with Game-Changing Public Relations*. "If you make beauty or baby products, for example, get in front of related issues, like safety and health, and become a thought leader in them," he says, "and be sure your company is in the forefront of protecting consumers." Doing so means you can influence and even frame debates instead of responding after the fact, when they can catch you unawares, according to Torossian.

Playing catch-up can be a potential nightmare for public and customer relations. If you've any doubt, ask any corporate communications chief at a large company if they've *ever* had a "happy" 3:00 a.m. phone call. "Leaders have a very real strategic interest in actively participating in events or potential controversies that relate directly to their bottom lines," says Torossian. Not becoming actively engaged with what outsiders are saying about your business can damage your reputation instead of creating opportunities that build value by addressing unmet consumer or shareholder concerns, needs, and preferences.

Leaders who engage their companies proactively and positively benefit economically—so yes, there is an advantage beyond the altruistic in becoming a good steward. Added bonus? You're a lot more knowledgeable about current events than the normal person, and you look incredibly smart at cocktail parties.

In order to do this, though, you have to listen to what's going on both in your community and globally so you can offer a rapid-fire response. Believe me, your constituents can mobilize quickly around a topic or a cause, which can be problematic for you if you've made them mad or if you haven't understood what's important to them. According to McKinsey & Company, since 1990, more than 100,000 new citizens' groups have been established around the world. A May 2006 report, "When Social Issues Become Strategic," notes, "The balance of power has shifted in favor of individuals and small single-issue groups increasingly armed with tools and tactics that can easily be deployed through the Internet."

In other words, when consumers or the press get wind of something about you that they don't like, you're screwed. (You know that little thing called Twitter, right? It was partly responsible for the Arab Spring.) That might be why, according to a study done by management consulting firm KPMG, a vast majority of top companies now report on their corporate social responsibility (CSR) activities as a matter of course. In the United States, KPMG found that while only 74 percent of companies reported their CSR activities in 2008, 83 percent of the top 100 businesses reported a CSR component in 2011. KPMG suggests a number of reasons for the increase in reporting despite the economic woes that have dogged many companies since the 2008 recession. Primary motivators for reporting on CSR include reputation and brand (67 percent), ethics (58 percent), employee motivation (44 percent), innovation and learning (44 percent), and risk management (35 percent).

JUST DON'T DO IT

In 2001 the multibillion-dollar sportswear company Nike admitted that it "blew it" when the BBC exposed the fact that the company employed children in Third World countries to produce its products and at extremely low wages. For years it had dealt with rumors of labor problems, but with the BBC story, bad press reached a head—campus protests, boycotts, and canceled contracts with university sports teams followed the revelations.

Company chairman Philip Knight was stung badly by the story of ten-year-olds toiling in sweatshop conditions in Pakistan and Cambodia and pleaded innocence, saying Nike was unaware that company labor standards (and US labor laws) were being broken. "Of all the issues facing Nike in workplace standards, child labor is the most vexing," he said in a corporate responsibility report. "Our age standards are the highest in the world: 18 for footwear manufacturing, 16 for apparel and equipment, our local standards whenever they are higher. But in some countries (Bangladesh and Pakistan, for example), those standards are next to impossible to verify, when records of birth do not exist or can be easily forged."

This report was actually a breakthrough for the company, an important departure from the more aggressive approach it took in the 1990s whenever reports of labor conditions in foreign factories surfaced. "Executives would issue denials, lash out at critics, and rush someone to the offending supplier's factory to put out the fire before it spread," wrote *Business Week*'s Aaron Bernstein in 2004. Since Knight publicly acknowledged the problem, Nike has done better—although it still has its critics, you don't see the kind of bad press about the sports manufacturer that was so common a decade ago.

Instead of reacting to the labor issues defensively, in the early 2000s Nike created an elaborate program in the more than 900 factories they use (but do not own) to produce products abroad. Nearly 100 staffers inspect several hundred of these factories every year, grade them on labor standards, and then work with managers to improve problems. Nike also allows random factory inspections by the Fair Labor Association (FLA). By 2011 the company seemed to have completely turned things around, and it received top recognition for sustainability reporting from the investment advocacy group Ceres and the Association of Chartered Certified Accountants.

Hannah Jones, vice president of sustainable business and innovation at Nike, is responsible for stewarding the company through global sustainability strategies. "Change is never easy to effect," she told GreenBiz.com reporter Maya Albanese in 2012. "When the focus is more on conflict and less on collaboration, we are *not* going to get where we need to go. . . . But in the case of companies—well, we need all of them to use their business models and resources to effect change. At Nike, we know we can leverage our innovation to help meet the demands and constraints of the world in which we operate."

Imagine for a second if this scandal had first broken in 2012 rather than 2000. The immediacy of social media would have caused a much, much bigger backlash than the one Nike first experienced. The company's quick thinking and commitment to change helped it overcome bad press in 2000, but in 2012, it would have been far more difficult to meet the demands of consumer backlash.

RIDE THE WINDS OF CHANGE

In today's world, people expect that companies will be good corporate citizens and that their leaders will exemplify stewardship by example. We want to feel that the products and services we buy are not only a good value, but also aren't damaging the earth or harming our families. We don't like it when companies engage in activities (like hiring kids to make T-shirts) that we consider unethical, distasteful, or just plain wrong. We're currently seeing this kind of reaction with Apple in the wake of reports about potentially unsafe conditions in factories overseas creating millions of iPads, iPods, and the like. While Apple has spectacular brand loyalty, which gives it some time to fix the problems, your company might not. Like listening, investing in assets that might be seen as only "reputational" aggravates some leaders who think it's a waste of money with no measurable payoff. It's not easy to look for social trends that could impact your business, so when such investment is difficult to justify to your stockholders, your board, or even yourself, understand this: it always comes back to dollars.

Sports gear maker Patagonia has long been at the forefront of responsible leadership. Company founder Yvon Chouinard has been an advocate of sustainable business practices ever since he started making mountain-climbing gear—he realized he could make equipment that did little or no damage to the mountains when climbers scaled them. He even wrote a book, *The Responsible Company,* about sustainability. A large part of the reason that Chouinard's leadership has made such an impact on business is because his company has so successfully used stewardship to enhance its bottom line—behemoths like Walmart, whose revenues exceed Patagonia's 800-fold, have looked to the company for advice about reducing packaging and water use in its world-renowned supply-chain system. The two companies have created the Sustainable Apparel Coalition, inviting other major brands, including Nike, Levi Strauss, Gap, and Adidas, to join them in crafting clear, quantifiable, and verifiable standards for environmentally responsible clothing production.

Walmart has taken other interesting steps in terms of stewardship. Sensing attitude changes toward food in its broadly middle-class customer base, as well as a shift in how the public and government view who is responsible for obesity and poor nutrition in this country, it initiated a program to reduce the sodium and sugar content in its Great Value brand food products over time. The reasoning behind the slow upgrade is that people don't notice gradual changes in flavor as much as they do dramatic ones. So, at least in theory, a gradual reduction in sodium will have less impact on sales than if Great Value taco shells, for example, were to go from 10 percent to 0 percent sodium content overnight. This is just one way in which Walmart has started reacting to the social and political changes in the world of food. The company even started carrying organic produce several years ago. Very, very smart.

In 2012 McDonald's started to put apples and a serving of French fries that was half of the original size in its Happy Meals instead of leaving the apples or fries option up to the parents or child. But the damage to their reputation was already done—the media had been talking about childhood obesity and the connection to fast and processed food since the 1990s. That was well before San Francisco banned toys from Happy Meals in 2010. McDonald's, which is usually a very innovative company, should have been ahead of the curve on this issue. It wasn't, but hey, at least it's a start. A late, half-gasped start, but a start nonetheless.

On the other hand, look at Whole Foods Market—its success provides clear evidence that listening to consumer concerns and acting on early signs of change can be quite profitable. In 1980 there were fewer than half a dozen natural food supermarkets in the United States. Four very small businesspeople in Austin, Texas, could see the tide turning in consumers' minds about food and health and decided the natural foods industry was ready for a supermarket format. Founders John Mackey (who leads the company today) and Renee Lawson Hardy, owners of Safer Way Natural Foods, and Craig Weller and Mark Skiles, owners of Clarksville Natural Grocery, started the original Whole Foods Market with a staff of 19 people. It was an immediate success.

Today there are more than 100 Whole Foods, including the one I go to near Columbus Circle in New York City, which is so busy that the store actually posts signs telling people the best time to shop. The company placed third on the US Environmental

Protection Agency's list of the "Top 25 Green Power Partners" and received the EPA Green Power Award in 2004 and 2005 and Partner of the Year award in 2006 and 2007. Don't get me wrong—Whole Foods does have its critics and naysayers, and occasional strange stories about them surface in the media, but the company works hard to respond to customer concerns. Mackey stands by a set of principles and continually evolves both the store's offerings and its sustainability practices to keep up with consumer and shareholder concerns.

SIZE DOESN'T MATTER

If you're a small enterprise and are thinking, "This isn't for me, I've got too much going on to worry about sustainability," think again. *Every* business, no matter its size, has to care about stewardship, whether they make it an actual part of their business plan (like Whole Foods, or Toyota with its Prius), or whether they focus outside it, as in charity work or community service. Local businesses in particular can have a positive impact on their communities and, through stewardship, engage customers in a unique and powerful way. It's not just about the benefits of networking and garnering good local press. Every robust business is built on the philosophy that doing good equals doing well. "Do anything, big or small, to make the world better. Just don't do nothing" sums it up well.

John Shegerian, CEO and founder of Electronic Recyclers International (electronicrecyclers.com) and 1800Recycling.com, has a unique business model. Ten percent of his employees are ex-cons who he hired in hopes of giving a second chance and, in many cases, a last chance. Through John's social entrepreneurship and positive attitude, Electronic Recyclers International has become the largest e-waste recycling company in the nation, with increasing revenues.

As the founder and CEO of One Stop Environmental (OSE, www.onestopenv.com), Shannon Riley is responsible for the leadership, strategy, and technical foundation of her full-service environmental company that specializes in federal and private environmental issues. Shannon also takes very seriously the responsibility of contributing to and improving her community. OSE has coordinated and aided in beautification projects in the Woodlawn area of Birmingham, Alabama, and OSE employees serve the local education system by volunteering in a weekly tutoring program at a local elementary school. In addition, Shannon started recycling programs at two neighborhood schools that educate students on the importance of recycling and provide recycling bins to the schools. OSE believes that when communities flourish, the company flourishes, and the balance sheets prove it: started in 1999 as an emergency response company, OSE has grown under Shannon's stewardship to be one of the premier full-service environmental companies in the United States.

Miraval Arizona Resort and Spa draws people from around the world not only for the luxury and pampering it provides, but also because it is a consciously sustainable and environmentally sound resort. The company recently partnered with "Mrs. Green," Gina Murphy-Darling, an Arizona environmental activist with a popular Tucson-based radio show. "Because we are a sustainable company, that partnership has earned us the respect of employees and many community members who may not normally think of staying with us because we are in their own backyard," says president Michael Tompkins.

BEING GOOD IS AN INVESTMENT

The keys to good stewardship are pretty simple, but they do require attention—which is why more than 150 of the world's largest companies have an executive-level (vice president or higher) sustainability officer focusing on stewardship and environmental issues. It can't just be a sideline anymore. Admittedly, there are some frustrations involved in practicing stewardship. It can consume a great deal of time, and you often have to wait a while to see results, which can be notoriously difficult to measure in dollars, unless sustainability is the product you're selling. Ignoring stewardship will be more costly in the long run, however. This is the direction in which business is headed and where it will be for the long term.

Consider the following when thinking about stewardship:

1. Put your social radar up—keep ahead of subtle changes in thinking and consumer behavior that will impact your business.
2. Show your stewardship authentically—in other words, work on programs that you actually care about, that have a logical connection to your business, and that are the acknowledged best practices of your industry.
3. Involve the community—not only by sharing information about what you're doing but also by listening to customer reactions and needs.

CONSERVING FOR FUN AND PROFIT

For a born-and-raised New York City kid who still lives in Manhattan and will never move, I'm surprisingly outdoorsy. I've trained for and run in the ING New York City Marathon countless times, done Ironman Triathlons, and am a licensed skydiver with more than 300 jumps to my name. At any rate, because of my penchant for sporting adventure (some would say insanity), I'm always on the lookout for my next fitness exploit and the best gear to get me through it. That's how I discovered REI (Recreational Equipment Inc.). The company, founded in 1938 as a members' cooperative, not only sells all sorts of great outdoor gear and clothing, including a house brand line of products, but also makes land conservation part of its business plan. That's a big reason why I'm a customer. The corporate vision, to promote outdoor activities while also maintaining nature, is integral to its success.

REI exemplifies how a company can make a real difference in the world, promote its environmental values to customers, and make a profit. REI stands behind everything they sell with a 100 percent satisfaction guarantee, which I love. More than that, REI donates millions of dollars to support conservation efforts nationwide and sends dedicated teams of volunteers—members, customers, and REI employees—to build trails, clean up beaches, restore local habitats, and carry out other environmental projects. By staying true to its missions and values, REI has consistently earned a place on *Fortune* magazine's list of the "100 Best Companies to Work For" every year since the rankings began in 1998.

> "We believe it is in the long-term interests of REI to preserve natural spaces, engaging people in playing outdoors and taking care of the environment."
> —Sally Jewell

You can still join the Kent, Washington–based privately held company for a $20 membership fee. For that modest sum, co-op members can vote for the company's board of directors and share in the company's profits through an annual refund check for their REI purchases. It's a structure that gives customers a feeling of involvement with the firm that's deeper than most retail relationships. And why wouldn't it? According to CEO Sally Jewell, the company paid a record dividend of $99.8 million to its 4.7 million active members in early 2011. It's worth it, in that REI has access to highly detailed information about members' purchasing habits.

This allows the company to target and pitch different kinds of merchandise to specific customers, and, as a result, it gets higher acceptance. According to *Forbes,* REI had revenues of $1.7 billion in 2010, a boost from $1.5 billion the year before.

Because of the close alignment between co-op members and REI's corporate values, its membership has contributed nearly three million hours of volunteer service in parks, recreation areas, and natural spaces across the country. With the board's support, the co-op dedicates 3 percent of its annual operating profits to facilitating and encouraging these activities.

Jewell, a former banking executive, took over the company in 2005, replacing Dennis Madsen, who spent his nearly 40-year career with the company. Jewell's banking experience helped bring focus to the aging company and reinvigorated its appeal to younger customers by finding ways to move the meter on the number of kids who participate in outdoor activities. "Our competitors are TV, video games, and kids who are overscheduled," Jewell told the *Seattle Times* in 2005. Without younger generations learning how to enjoy the great outdoors, REI wouldn't survive—and without an outdoors to enjoy, there would be no place to send kids who could become customers.

Focusing REI on sustainability efforts, including reducing its energy consumption, and corporate social responsibility, such as paying close attention to the overseas working conditions of its manufacturers, is a no-brainer for Jewell. "We believe it is in the long-term interests of REI to preserve natural spaces, engaging people in playing outdoors and taking care of the environment. To be serving outdoor enthusiasts for 100 years from now and beyond, you have to have outdoor enthusiasts, and you have to have the outdoors as well," Jewell said at an Institute for Corporate Ethics business roundtable in 2009.

By placing the environment at the top of REI's business agenda, Jewell shifted the company's stewardship efforts away from what she has described as a "random acts of kindness" approach toward a more calculated "way we do business" plan. In addition to reducing its carbon emissions and setting a very aggressive goal to bring its landfill waste to zero by 2020, REI joined with other businesses to create the Outdoor Industry Association (OIA) Fair Labor Toolkit. The Toolkit provides a resource for companies looking for ways to ensure proper working conditions for its supplier factories. In 2006 REI also collaborated with Forest Ethics, a nonprofit environmental organization, after its paper purchasing policies received a D+ grade from the group, which aims to protect endangered forests by exposing corporations that destroy them.

Aside from giving to numerous conservation programs and encouraging members and employees to volunteer, REI also has a tremendous local community outreach program wherever its stores are located (80 percent of sales are from retail operations, with the other 20 percent coming from online sales). Jewell has ensured that REI is a good neighbor by sponsoring many outdoor events, family activities, and a range of classes—from canoeing and biking to nature photography. In September 2012 the retailer announced it had granted more than $3.9 million this year to national and local organizations offering volunteer programs in the outdoors. It's a practice that has paid off in numerous ways, not the least of which is in profits. In 2011 REI reported that sales grew by 8.4 percent to $1.8 billion.

WHEN SPINNING YOUR WHEELS TAKES YOU PLACES

If you're running a smaller business—you know, the kind that doesn't ring up more than a billion in sales—and you're still not convinced that stewardship is a trait that you can afford to cultivate, consider SPIN! Neapolitan Pizza, a small Kansas City–based restaurant chain. I might add that anytime I get to talk about pizza, I consider it a win. But SPIN! Neapolitan Pizza is something special, even though co-owners Gail and Richard Lozoff and Edwin Brownell operate four units and only plan to open two more. SPIN! Neapolitan Pizza has won numerous national and local awards for its food and was named a finalist for the Greater Kansas City Chamber's Small Business of the Year. Their story demonstrates how stewardship through community outreach can be an inexpensive and highly effective way to build both reputation and customer awareness.

SPIN! also has an outstanding reputation as a great place to work: many of the 150 employees have worked for SPIN! for several years, bucking the traditional high turnover typically seen in restaurants. Those who begin working while in school often continue to work part-time after they graduate and get full-time jobs. The Lozoffs and Brownell have created a business with a unique hybrid service concept, an eclectic rotating roster of wines priced well below traditional restaurant prices, and national award–winning artisan food made from fresh ingredients and recipes created in collaboration with a James Beard Award–winning chef—but without the gourmet price. A James Beard chef at a pizza restaurant! As a privately held company, it does not reveal financial figures, but its growth and award-winning food demonstrate its success. The owners will admit that their planned growth wouldn't be possible if the restaurants weren't paying off. Pretty cool for a pizza place.

SPIN! has an impressive record in community service programs—far beyond what is typical of a business this size. "When we started the company in 2005, we had a vision of restaurants that had a local feel and that were truly part of the communities they were in," says Gail. "We started by supporting community groups. Being in the food business makes that very easy, because every local organization needs either food or auction items. It sounds a little silly to say this, but we do not turn anyone down."

It doesn't sound silly to me—donating products or services is a great way for a new or small business to ingratiate itself with the locals while also practicing good citizenship.

"We reserve dollars every year for these events, and we go out of the way to make them successful for organizers and participants," says Gail. "For instance, our local Junior League did a bicycle drive to get gently used bikes to inner city kids. They asked if SPIN! locations could be used as drop-offs for the bikes and to provide food for the main event, presentation of the bikes. The answer was an immediate yes and yes." SPIN! has a large database of customers, and the company jumped at the chance to tell them about the bike drive. According to Richard Lozoff, the "SPIN! Club" has 60,000 registered members who receive weekly emails about upcoming rides and other events. For the drive, SPIN! partnered with a bike shop to do repairs on donated cycles. "The cool thing about our database in terms of the community is that when an organization comes to us for help publicizing an event, we have a conduit to get the message out," says Richard.

So why was SPIN! so on board with the bicycle drive? Because it fits with the brand, for one thing. "First of all, our name conjures up wheels, as does our logo. The whole idea of the restaurant is to combine the fantasy of Italy, pizza, wine, and bicycling," says Gail. "It's a big theme for us—it's apparent in our logo, and we have bike imagery on our marketing materials. The health aspects of it are crucial too—we're proud of our food's nutritionals, which we provide on our website. It all works together."

> "The cool thing about our database in terms of the community is that when an organization comes to us for help publicizing an event, we have a conduit to get the message out."
>
> —Richard Lozoff

More than that, the restaurants support community cycling in the Kansas City area by sponsoring weekly bike rides that gather at restaurant locations. "We hired trained cyclists to help people who have not been on bikes in a long time to get used to biking again. We encourage families to come and use the rides as a group exercise. They gather for pizza at SPIN!, and we give riders a percentage off their meal," Gail says. The rides are popular—between 75 and 100 people turn up for every scheduled event.

Because there are so many other fund-raising cycling events in Kansas City, SPIN!'s owners promote as many events as they can to their database. If it's got something to do with biking, SPIN! wants to be there. "We are known as the leader in Kansas City biking, and people wear our jerseys all over the city, and that becomes a moving billboard," says Richard. At one recent large citywide fund-raising ride, the Tour de Barbeque, which raises money for cancer, SPIN! had more than 100 people wearing its jerseys at once. "That put us out in the community in a guerilla way, which is crucial for us since we don't do a lot of advertising, and advertising is so fragmented anyway, unless you use social and digital media. So we promote through biking and our guests," he says. But does it pay? "Some of the results are measurable," says Gail. "There is certainly an increase in our revenue on the days we have bike events, because they bring in a lot of guests. Half of the people who come for the ride stay for food, so it's very easy to justify from a financial perspective. But what the rides do for the brand and our connection to the community and relationships with customers and other organizations is priceless."

Another community outreach SPIN! has devised is promoting local singer-songwriters in their restaurants. Its "Folk on the Patio" program showcases musicians and offers free live performances throughout the summer. A lot of restaurants don't adopt a similar approach because of ASCAP rules that require performers to pay royalties for songs used. That's why SPIN! requires singers to perform only their own music—a solution that turned a problem into an asset. "The community can get to know the city's local talent—and it's another reason for people to gather at the restaurant," says Gail.

This kind of local thinking is one reason that Gail, Richard, and Ed believe they suffer less turnover than other restaurants. "Employees are attracted to us because they know about our connection to our community. We're not here just to run a business—we want to contribute to the well-being of our communities. If you ask our servers why they like SPIN!, they will tell you it's because we care about the community and the people. We get our people involved in community events, and they volunteer in events we participate in. It makes them feel good that they are welcome to join our bike rides," says Gail.

Finally, SPIN! does what it can to use local purveyors for some of its pizza toppings. The meats it uses come from local companies, and some produce is locally grown. The restaurant's wine program, which is one of its unique features, is put together with the help of local wine merchants. These are small things, but they add up in terms of SPIN!'s reputation and good standing in Kansas City.

These are all simple, inexpensive efforts that any company can make—being a good steward does not mean spending millions on nonprofits or sponsoring big international events. Charity really does start at home, and if you're leading a regional business, it's time to think about what you could be doing to make a contribution to the community. What fits with your brand and your own interests? That's a good place to start.

Seriously—why wouldn't you do this?!

SUMMARY OF KEY POINTS

Good stewards

- Are, first and foremost, good neighbors—it all starts where you live;
- Choose stewardship that fits with and reflects well on their business;
- Keep track of trends so they can get in front of them, not follow behind;
- Constantly seek to improve upon their stewardship efforts; and
- Understand that investment in stewardship is an investment in their reputation and longevity.

7

TRAIT #5

360 Loyalty

"Loyalty to petrified opinion never yet broke a chain or freed a human soul."

—Mark Twain

"Loyalty? I have a cat. He's surprisingly loyal."

—Peter Shankman

Loyalty is one of the most complex traits to deal with, hands down. On the surface, the textbook definition of loyalty—unwavering commitment to something or someone—sounds wonderful. But then so did the concept of a cute blond kid singing—and that gave us Justin Bieber. See, over time loyalty can actually transform into a weakness when a blind allegiance is given to a bad idea or to a person. For instance, loyalty to founding partners or colleagues you grew up with can be a liability. At some point, you might have to change out team members who are no longer performing as required or who are not changing with the business. That's not easy. Not doing so is worse—inaction in the name of loyalty can ruin a business and end up putting a lot of good people out of work. It's a variation of the Peter Principle, which says that each worker will rise to his or her highest level of incompetence and will be unable to move up or down once there. On the other hand, promoting 360 Loyalty to the workplace and the business can engender reciprocal treatment from good employees. Likewise, working through and believing in ideas that don't always take off in the first five minutes can have a tremendous payoff.

Make no mistake—leaders bestow loyalty. It is within your power and discretion, and that's what makes it so tricky. Even businesses with high percentages of employee participation and organizational engagement aren't democracies. True, many decisions are delegated to subordinates, and some can be made by popular choice. But at the end of the day, a business is a form of dictatorship, benign in some cases, corrosive in others. Of course there are regulations, and owners and CEOs have to follow the law or face the consequences, but leaders still have enormous freedom of choice and action. They can distribute bonuses unfairly and under the radar of competing employees; implement unpopular policies; and play favorites with divisions, departments, and employees. There's a lot of leeway, which is why it's easy to get confused about loyalty—and to get it wrong.

Great leaders are loyal to what works for the whole company and for all good employees. They refrain from personal or stubborn loyalties to both pet projects that are doomed to fail and pet people who are ineffective and perhaps even destructive on the job. 360 Loyalty has the advantage of encouraging you and others in your company to continually consider the big picture and the mission of the company and determine how to maximize profits, innovation, and market share. Is this (*fill in the blank*) going to be good for the strength and health of the organization? If you waver from yes (the correct answer), you are being disloyal to the company and its employees, both good and bad. That will hurt.

WHY LOYALTY IS SO TOUGH TO PIN DOWN

There are many examples of situations in which sticking with a person or an idea pays off—they're often used as ammunition by people who can't or don't want to give up on a person or an idea. Here are a couple.

When the late Tom Watson Jr. was chief executive of IBM in the early 1960s, he called a young executive to his office after the man had lost $10 million in a failed and highly risky venture. Having gotten wind of Watson's legendary temper, the man assumed he was about to be fired and beat Watson to the punch by tendering his resignation.

"Fire you? You've got to be kidding," Watson is reported to have replied. "Hell, I spent $10 million educating you. I just want to be sure you learned the right lessons." I'd say that showed great loyalty to both an employee who had been identified as promising and to the core purpose of the company, which was to "THINK" and constantly develop businesses that would provide growth. When you're trying to build a business that will appeal to customers, you're going to make mistakes along the way. If the mistake provides valuable insights that you actually act on, it was worth it.

In August 1999 Tony Hsieh (who I'm proud to call a friend) invested $500,000 in what was universally considered to be a very bad idea: an online shoe store. Plus, he called it Zappos, which doesn't exactly scream *shoes*. About six months later, after the dot-com crash, Zappos was broke. In October 2000 Hsieh had to lay off half of his staff. Undeterred, he paid himself an annual salary of $24 and sold his San Francisco loft to buy a warehouse in Kentucky. He kept plugging away at selling shoes over the Internet—not discounted, but completely guaranteed in terms of customer service and satisfaction. The customer service aspect of his business model started to resonate with consumers. By the end of 2002 Zappos's sales had hit $32 million, but the company had yet to turn a profit.

In March 2004 Hsieh moved the Zappos headquarters to Las Vegas, where there was a bounty of experienced call-center workers. By August 2005 Zappos had sales of $370 million but still no profit—nevertheless, Amazon chairman and CEO Jeff Bezos offered to buy it. Hsieh turned him down, feeling that the sale could put the company's unique culture at risk. In December 2007 Zappos topped $100 million in monthly merchandise sales, ending the year with revenue of $840 million and, for the very first time, a profit. Hsieh finally gave in to Bezos and allowed Amazon to buy Zappos for $1.2 billion in November 2009.

Okay, you might be wondering if Zappos doesn't prove that hanging on to pet ideas is worthwhile. Every venture capitalist thought the idea sucked, but Hsieh's single-mindedness was visionary; he didn't let naysayers or financial losses allow him to throw in the towel. That's very true. And Hsieh did have to fire people, and he did have to spend his own money to fund the company as a start-up. Still, he kept at it. And if things had not worked out for Hsieh, Zappos could be a footnote in those annual "Ideas that Failed" lists that business magazines like to publish.

But if you look at the trajectory of the business—from 1999 to 2007, when it turned a profit—eight years is not too bad. I'd say it's pretty average. And the company was generating sales, breaking even, and paying its bills before it made money. Consider that its buyer, Amazon, didn't make a profit until 2003, its *ninth* year of operations and seven years after going public. I'd argue that if Hsieh were still trying to sell shoes today and weren't making any money, we might want to consider him blindly and badly loyal to Internet shoe selling.

The problem is CEOs or leaders who buy into an idea and can't get out of it when it's obvious that it will not work. It's one thing to try something and then cut your losses when it fails. It's another to keep banging your head against the wall and bringing everyone around you crashing in with you. Your loyalty to an idea is hanging on too long when it starts limiting your company's

potential growth, demoralizing workers, annoying clients or customers, bleeding money, and causing you to avoid market input
that might actually save your ass.

Staying the course in terms of your business model because
"that's the way it's always done" isn't loyalty—it's suicide. I want
to tell you a story told to me by a brilliant boss I was once lucky
enough to have. It's about baboons.

> Week 1: Place six baboons in a room. On the ceiling fan, place a
> banana. Every time a baboon tries to reach for a banana, spray
> all the baboons with an ice-cold shower. It doesn't matter who
> reaches for the banana; all baboons get sprayed. After a week
> of research, no baboon in the room will attempt to reach for a
> banana.

> Week 2: Take out one of the baboons and introduce a new one
> to the room. The first thing that the newcomer will attempt is
> to reach for the banana on the ceiling fan. However, he will
> deal with great force and intimidation from the other baboons,
> since they, of course, know that his attempt will be followed by
> the ice-cold shower. After a while, the newcomer will stop at-
> tempting to reach for the banana, since any time he does it, he's
> beaten up by five old-time baboons.

> Week 3: Take yet another original baboon out of the pack and
> introduce a new one. Observe the same scenario. Also, observe
> the newcomer from Week 2 admonishing the new baboon not
> to reach for the banana.

> Week 4: Same thing. Now you've got three baboons from Week
> 1 and three new baboons.

> Week 5: Same thing.

> Week 6: Same thing.

Week 7: This is where it gets interesting. A brand new baboon is introduced, and none of the original baboons who were in Week 1 remain. However, observe how aggressively the new-comer will be "advised" when he tries to reach for the banana. Notice that none of the baboons currently in the room is aware of the ice-cold shower.

So why don't they reach for the banana?
Because that's the way they've always done it.

Eastman Kodak, founded in 1880, was the leader of the film and camera industries until 1984. That year Fujifilm started to sell film similar to Kodak's, but they charged 20 percent less for it, and consumers responded positively. Over the next few years, other film brands entered the market, and they also undercut Kodak on price.

When Kay R. Whitmore took over Kodak in 1990, he brought with him a loyalty to the brand's luster as the gold standard in picture taking. He thought the strength of the brand would be enough to overcome changes in the marketplace—and he kept prices high. But he was wrong. The company was able to sustain profitability for about 12 years, but Whitmore's stubborn loyalty to the idea of Kodak ensured that the company lost out on the film, film paper, and camera markets that were opening up and becoming more price competitive.

Kodak knew about digital photography in 1981, but it had grown very attached to the 60 percent-plus profit margins on its traditional film, chemicals, and paper. Whitmore mistakenly saw digital technology as an enhancement to the "real" camera business, not as the next wave of consumer photography. The *New York Times* reported that when a Kodak researcher invented a key piece of digital technology, management's reaction was, "That's cute—but don't tell anyone about it." With encouragement like that, it's no wonder innovators in the field didn't think of Kodak first when pursuing new opportunities.

The wide popularity and increasing affordability of digital photography battered demand for traditional film, squeezing Kodak's business so much that in 2003 the company said that it would stop investing in its longtime product. They just came too late to the digital game. The name no longer resonated with consumers, who had moved on to other more modern and technologically advanced brands. Between 1976, when it had 90 percent of the film market, and the mid-2000s, Kodak lost 75 percent of its market value and shed more than two-thirds of its workforce. It tried a number of turnaround strategies and cost-cutting efforts, but the company—which between 2004 and 2012 had reported only one full year of profit—ran out of cash. In January 2012 the 131-year-old film pioneer filed for bankruptcy protection.

Let's go back to Tom Watson Jr. for a minute—because he had an innate sense of 360 Loyalty. In August 1987 Watson published an essay in *Fortune* magazine discussing his career at IBM. The idea of loyalty inevitably came up. "It took me a number of years to realize that a CEO has to spot-check decisions made by his subordinates," he wrote. He described an incident in which some plant managers had started a chain letter with the idea that one manager would write to five others and they would write to five more and so on, and everyone would send money back to a name on the list. Eventually, they ran out of managers, and they started sending the letters to rank-and-file employees, who felt under pressure to send money to the managers at the top of the list.

"I got a letter of complaint about this and brought it to the attention of the boss of the division. I expected him to say, at a minimum, 'We've got to fire a couple of guys. I'll handle it.' Instead he simply said, 'Well, it was a mistake.' I couldn't persuade him to fire anybody," wrote Watson, who was fairly young in his career at the time and didn't have the clout to make his subordinate fire anyone. "Now you could admire him for defending his team, but I think there is a time when integrity should take the rudder from team loyalty." While he thought the manager was capable, he also felt he had a detrimental blind spot that hindered his career.

"If it had happened a few years later, I would have fired the managers involved myself. I did this in perhaps a dozen cases when managers broke rules of integrity. Each time, I overruled a lot of people who argued that we should merely demote the man, or that the operation would fall apart without him. The company was invariably better off for the decision and the example, but the decisions were lonely," Watson wrote. Making the right decisions for a business can be unpopular, which is one reason that leaders avoid making them. You can make a strong argument that the choice *not* to fire the bad eggs was disloyal to the rank-and-file workers and honest managers who either felt pressured by the chain letters or weren't involved in sending them.

The funny thing is, showing myopic loyalty eventually produces disloyalty among the majority of employees who aren't benefiting from it, especially those who are really good at their jobs but are overlooked. You can and will lose them—either they'll "check out" or walk out. Corporate Leadership Council research found that employees who are the most committed perform 20 percent better and are 87 percent less likely to leave the organization than those who aren't. Human resource research indicates that replacement costs are 30 to 50 percent of the annual salary of entry-level employees, 150 percent of the salary of middle-level employees, and up to 400 percent of the salary of specialized, high-level employees.

THE BEST WAY TO SHOW LOYALTY? "YOU'RE FIRED."

Who or what exactly are you being loyal to when you retain a poor employee toward whom you have personal feelings—whether your loyalty is based on history, friendship, or gratitude for some previous help that person might have given you? If you've done what you can to intervene and improve that person's performance and it hasn't worked, do yourself, your other workers, and that employee a favor and let him or her go.

"Many poor performers thrive in new environments but don't have the courage to make the move on their own. Dismissal can be a catalyst for new growth for them, too," says Robert Sher, the founding principal of CEO to CEO, a firm that advises chief executives of mid-market companies that are navigating major changes in their business or marketplace. He tells the story of Melanie Dulbecco, the 20-year CEO of R. Torre & Co., which makes the Torani line of syrup flavorings. In 2007 growth flattened, and Dulbecco knew her long-standing executive team couldn't take the San Francisco–based company to the next level. "In an orderly and respectful manner, she changed out the team. R. Torre has since returned to double-digit annual growth," says Sher.

At Zappos, a company known for its freewheeling culture and nice CEO, new hires are put through a vigorous four-week onboarding training, which serves as an extended test of employees' "fit" with the firm. And the company doesn't shy away from getting rid of people who don't make the cut at any time during their employment. "We're slow to hire, but we're quick to fire when it comes to that," says Lyndsey Allen, a recruiter for Zappos. "Most people get caught in the training class, and they don't realize it's still a test, so [they] let their guard down."

Even after the onboarding period is over, an employee can be fired at any time, because Nevada, where the call center is based, is a "right-to-work" state, meaning a worker can be terminated at any time, except for performance-related issues. Hiring for skills and the right personality fit for the culture is loyalty to the other employees. And Hsieh proves it with low turnover rates: in 2011 Zappos experienced a voluntary turnover rate of just 8 percent.

NURTURING EMPLOYEE GROWTH IS
LOYALTY THAT PAYS DIVIDENDS

So what kind of loyalty should you show employees? The kind that makes them enthusiastic about your mission, encourages them to work hard, and invests in their career to your benefit. Don't hinder the professional development of good workers at the expense of keeping those who consistently falter on board. Finding ways to motivate good employees and identifying and nurturing those who have the potential to bring skills, knowledge, and ideas to the table is not only loyal—it makes financial sense.

It costs more and works out less successfully to hire someone from the outside than it does to develop talented internal candidates, according to recent research. There is talent ripe for growth in your ranks. Unfortunately, according to a May 2012 story in *Knowledge@Wharton,* employee loyalty is at historically low levels, despite unpleasant economic conditions. The story cites MetLife's tenth annual survey of employee benefits, trends, and attitudes, released in March 2012, that put employee loyalty at a seven-year low. This survey found that one in three employees planned to voluntarily leave his or her job by the year's end. A 2011 Careerbuilder.com report found that 76 percent of full-time workers, while not actively looking for a new job, would leave their current workplace in a heartbeat if a better opportunity presented itself. The report noted that other workplace loyalty studies confirmed that the average company loses from 20 to 50 percent of its employee base annually.

While people want to talk to their boss about their future prospects, most executives don't discuss career development with their employees, including top talent. What a wasted opportunity! If your best and brightest feel as if they can go places in your company, they'll be more likely to show you loyalty by sticking around and doing a great job.

External candidates cost more to recruit than the person sitting down the hallway. A March 2012 study from the University of Pennsylvania's Wharton School, entitled "Why External Hires Get Paid More, and Perform Worse, than Internal Staff," found that external hires were paid about 18 percent more than internal employees in equivalent roles but fared worse in performance reviews during their first two years on the job. Hiring managers can be seduced by an outsider's interesting résumé or the idea of injecting some new life or a new point of view into a company. But Matthew Bidwell, one of the researchers on the study, said companies often underestimate how difficult and costly it can be to integrate new people into a company's culture. They don't hit the ground running as fast as someone who's come up through the ranks.

Some companies have started to recognize the value their employees offer and are acting on it. In the old days, employees would feel guilty and slightly furtive about looking around in their company for another job. That's changing. The networking leader Cisco Systems Inc. developed an internal career program in 2010 called Talent Connection that human resources uses to identify qualified employees who may not actively be looking for another job in the company, but who may be a perfect and beneficial fit. Talent Connection helps the company respond more quickly to talent demands than it could by using an outside recruiter to conduct a search, prescreen candidates, and set up in-house interviews (and remember, professional headhunters often charge hefty fees).

According to Mark Hamberlin, a Cisco vice president of global staffing, Talent Connection has saved the company "several million dollars" in search-firm fees and other recruiting costs.

Internal candidates filled nearly 80 percent of open positions, and the time to fill a position dropped by an average of 22 days during the ten-week pilot program. Feedback from both candidates and managers indicated a high level of satisfaction with the new process. Meanwhile, employee surveys show that workers' satisfaction with career development has risen by nearly 20 percentage points.

One of Google CEO Larry Page's management mantras seems to be "Build your team, avoid bureaucracy." For many years, Page insisted on being involved in every hiring decision at Google. Many of the first employees came from the University of Michigan or Stanford University, where he and co-founder Sergey Brin met while in graduate school. Some of the first hires have gone on to start their own companies, but many have remained with Google—three out of six people promoted to lead Google's major product divisions in 2011 were also part of the initial group of ten employees Page hired in 1998. Yet even as Page and his team of recruiters actively seek thousands of talented graduates to join their ranks, he has also made an effort to streamline middle management, reduce bureaucracy, and open more growth opportunities to existing employees.

In 2011, Google replaced its internal job board with Magnet, a site that gives workers detailed information about internal career paths and encourages mobility across departments and projects. Employees can use the system to tag themselves as looking for new opportunities, and their information is then accessible to in-house recruiters or managers who need to fill new positions. Managers have less of a tendency to hoard talented people when they know that workers can put themselves on the open market internally—if they do lose one of their own to another department, they know that the individual is staying with the company, and that they have equal access to other talent that can fill the open position.

Booz Allen Hamilton chairman and CEO Dr. Ralph W. Shrader has been at the helm of the management and technology consultancy since 1999 and has led the firm through a period of significant growth and strategic realignment, the spin-off of its old commercial management consulting business, a major private equity investment, and an initial public offering. Shrader says he looks for people who are very technically capable—the first sign that they'll eventually become part of the company's "inner circle" of decision and strategy makers. So "key number one" to advancement at Booz Allen Hamilton is to attain and maintain a level of professional mastery at your job.

In part to help employees develop mastery, the company created an internal recruiting system called Inside First that allows in-house recruiters who specialize in each of the business's practice areas to identify the right internal candidates for open jobs. Managers and employees also have access to a database of job openings and staff profiles and are actively encouraged to use it. Each business unit has a recruiter who acts as a career coach and a matchmaker. The company, which employs about 25,000 people, filled about 30 percent of open positions with internal hires in 2012 using the system, which is 20 percent more than it did in 2010, according to Lucy Sorrentini, a principal in people services at the firm. She also says the company has found that it is more efficient and easier for insiders than brand-new hires to immerse themselves in new jobs because they understand the culture and often have good working relationships with other team members. All of which makes mastery a more reachable goal.

The development and cultivation of internal hires is not only working on staff and management levels; new research shows that chief executives hired from outside a company are twice as likely to be forced out as those promoted from within. According to consultants Booz & Company's twelfth annual CEO Succession Study, released in May 2012, which analyzed the 2,500 largest publicly traded companies around the world, between 2009 and 2011, 35 percent of "outsider" CEOs were dismissed, compared with just 19 percent of "insider" CEOs during that same period. Insider CEOs tend to hold on to their jobs for five years before they're dismissed, nearly a year longer than outsider CEOs. Experts say outsiders are probably more likely to be ousted because they're less familiar with a company's inner workings. The theory is that insiders understand the company and know how to effectively communicate changes to strategy—they have built up the currency of trust, which they can spend when changes need to be made. There's more acceptance of both modest and sweeping changes among workers when they come from someone they know, whereas the same changes implemented by an outsider will meet more resistance.

There's another benefit to cultivating insiders to CEO status— on average, they deliver better returns for shareholders. To determine differences, the Booz & Company study analyzed the market performance of companies with a chief executive departure between 2009 and 2011 and calculated the company's returns during that CEO's tenure. Companies with an insider boss outperformed their respective stock market index by 4.4 percent, while those with an outsider outperformed their index by 0.5 percent.

THE CIRCULAR VIEW

The keys to 360 Loyalty are straightforward enough, but they do require self-examination and a mental checklist. You're not being a "nice guy" when you make emotionally based decisions, so you have to ask yourself, "Am I keeping this underperforming employee because I feel sorry for them or because I like them or have 'known them forever'?" You're not doing anyone any favors if you are. Is a struggling idea or business unit worth continued investment because you're determined to prove it's right and being right is more important than anything else? If so, it's time to let go. True loyalty is investing in the people and ideas that are going to help everyone prosper and grow. Consider the following when thinking about 360 Loyalty:

- Give employees opportunities and tools to master their jobs and use their talents and knowledge for mutual benefits.
- Respect good employees' work and show your loyalty to them with policies and rewards that reflect your understanding of their contribution to the business.
- Show all employees that supporting the business's mission by doing a good job and mastering skills grows sales and creates a richer, more beneficial experience for them.
- Encourage criticism of the "way we've always done it" as a check against hanging on to policies, procedures, and philosophies that no longer serve the company's bottom line and market.
- Publicize mistakes—*including your own*—and what lessons were learned from them.
- Identify those workers who may not be carrying their weight—intervene, but if it doesn't help, cut your losses for everyone's sake.

> "The most decisive factor for our success was how drastically we were able to transform our businesses when digitalization occurred."
> —Shigetaka Komori

PICTURE LOYALTY TO THE MARKET

A closer look at one of Kodak's winning competitors demonstrates the beauty and benefits of loyalty to the market as opposed to loyalty to tradition or an idea. Fujifilm came on the American scene in 1984 and won market share very quickly, in part by undercutting Kodak's prices on film. Fujifilm's success is a clear example of why developing products and businesses that serve the changing marketplace is much wiser than selling old products via brand recognition. Shigetaka Komori, Fujifilm's president and CEO until June 2012, when he became chairman, came to the firm in 1963, a time when Kodak was the leader in film and photography. He looked on the competing American company with great respect and admiration.

Fujifilm, like Kodak, was also aware in the early 1980s of the growing technological developments in digital photography, but, like Kodak, it was still enjoying the enormous profits it earned from selling film. While Fujifilm did invest in digital technologies and tried to diversify into new areas, the people running the very profitable film division had the most clout (where there's money—there's power). Like the film people at Kodak, they were loath to admit that digital photography would likely dominate the consumer market in the not-too-distant future. Protecting turf and jobs can override concerns for the direction of a business and the marketplace—a knee-jerk reaction that should not be mistaken for loyalty. Job protection has short-term and narrow benefits that in the long term usually don't pan out too well. It's safe to assume that the natural pain of transition was risky for the film people—they may have feared mastering the new skills necessary to survive. That's why it's so important to educate employees and develop their skills as the market changes.

In 2000 Fujifilm's strategy was based on the idea that film would go through a gradual decline over 15 to 20 years. Instead, the free fall of film sales happened quickly starting in the early 2000s. In just ten years, film profits at Fujifilm went from 60 percent to nothing. Komori understood that his company had to develop a team of employees who had mastery over the new technology and who could also develop new businesses. "We re-defined the business. In times of massive digital photography, the classic film almost disappeared from the market. Just look what happened to our former competitors," Komori told THEME, a reference site for photography, in May 2012.

As sales from film developing and printing dwindled, Komori saw an opportunity to shift developing services to self-service printing kiosks in stores. After all, people still wanted to have "hard" copies of some of the hundreds of pictures digital cameras made so easy to take. The paper and developing chemicals—as well as the printing technology—could all belong to Fujifilm if they had the people to develop the technology for them in-house. And so they did.

Fujifilm made a deal with Walmart to provide kiosks for self-service printing in its camera department. That partnership gave Fujifilm huge visibility and market share. As a result, Fujifilm dominates almost 40 percent of the photofinishing market in America, compared to Kodak's 15 percent share, according to IBISWorld, a research firm. Komori understood that the kiosk technology had applications beyond helping Mr. and Mrs. Potatohead develop pics of Johnny's soccer game. Its digital-imaging division was able to develop uses for the medical and cosmetic industries.

As a result, Fujifilm became a much more diversified company than Kodak—mainly by becoming loyal to the market and developing in-house people who could innovate quickly enough to save them from the same fate Kodak has suffered. Fujifilm saw digital technologies as an opportunity to diversify and parlayed its chemical expertise into new industries like health care and cosmetics. According to Komori, "The most decisive factor [for the company's success] was how drastically we were able to transform our businesses when digitalization occurred." The longer-term vision necessitated a big investment—but it was an investment in people and development, not marketing, so even though the initial cost damaged the firm's short-term profits, it paid off in the long run. "We have more 'pockets' and 'drawers' in our company," he told THEME, as a way of saying that diversification of existing and new technologies gives them many options and revenue streams.

Fujifilm remains highly competitive in the digital camera, lens, and photography book markets. They also produce office printers and other equipment. In repositioning the company through making specific purchases and investing 6 to 8 percent of its revenue in research and development, Komori oversees six business areas that have strong growth potential: medical systems, graphic systems, optical devices, office communications, digital imaging, and functional materials—areas that are all, in one way or another, connected with film technology.

Ironically, the rate of decline in film sales actually started to slow in 2012, according to Fujifilm. Gabriel DeCosta, product manager for Fuji's film division, told TechRadar that it was not all doom and gloom, and that the division had plenty to celebrate. "We're still profitable with our film, and while we are still seeing a decline, it is not as aggressive as it was six months ago. We're not entirely sure why, it could be to do with Kodak's decline, or it could be thanks to the resurgence in retro cameras," he said. So it's not that you want to completely throw out old successes as your loyalties shift; you just have to rethink their place in the scheme of things.

SUMMARY OF KEY POINTS

360 Loyalty

- Allows for and encourages professional growth of employees;
- Provides flexibility for motivated, productive workers;

- Lets employees fail and ensures that everyone learns the lessons within the failure;
- Does not allow the business to be bogged down by bad ideas or underperforming employees; and
- Makes decisions based on the philosophy that if it's good for business, it's good for everyone.

8

TRAIT #6

Glass-Half-Full POV

"I always like to look on the optimistic side of life, but I am realistic enough to know that life is a complex matter."

—Walt Disney

have an old friend, a restaurateur of sorts, who started a chain of local taco and beer joints in his hometown, a middle-size city in the Midwest. Jack (not his real name) was always über-confident, a trait I used to admire in him. The first taco spot was a hit from the get-go, so Jack's self-described abilities as an entrepreneur and a trendsetter were confirmed. It made perfect sense that after that initial success he would expand the business.

Jack bought other storefronts and acquired the spaces of failed restaurants and installed his taquerías in them. He opened four new places in 18 months. Two of the five restaurants struggled from the day they opened. Jack started implementing changes in the sluggish venues, using marketing strategies that worked in the successful ones. When his managers suggested that what worked in one neighborhood wouldn't necessarily work in another, he listened to them but ultimately decided *he* was right. "These managers don't know the business anywhere near as well as me," he said. "They're just not doing their jobs well."

He was so invested in his own view of what would work that he couldn't see that his ideas weren't meeting expectations. Jack just refused to admit that different locations required different strategies—ironic, because thinking you can "educate the market" is really a rookie entrepreneurial mistake. He was in love with his formula, the one that had worked in a specific market. But as the two restaurants continued to spiral downward (and sucked money, time, and resources from the two that were performing), he couldn't rally his troops, no matter how hard he thought he was trying. He'd give pep talk after pep talk, but he couldn't inspire confidence in his employees to save his life. His cheerleading came across as completely hollow, style with no substance. Eventually, Jack had to shut down all five restaurants because the two failing establishments had sucked all of his resources dry.

As Jack's bank account took a major hit, his ego, unfortunately, was stronger than ever. Even after the restaurant failure, he insisted he was right; it was the customers who were wrong, the economy that sucked, the cost of products and labor that were too high. Had he gotten into a car accident, he would have blamed the car. I started looking at his confidence and personality in a different light. Jack didn't have a magical optimistic worldview that could overcome any obstacle; instead, his excessive and harmful self-confidence and pessimism toward everything outside of himself made for a weird and destructive combination. Ultimately, Jack was what I call a GHEP—a glass-half-empty person. Yin and yang run amok. Jack saw himself as the genius, convinced of his abilities and rightness, and just as certain of his detractors' wrongness. He looked at the world with a high degree of pessimism, and, as such, his life was never as perfect as he felt himself to be. And Jack had hubris—the overwhelming pride that often causes irrational and harmful behavior.

CAN OPTIMISM BACKFIRE?

So here's the thing. While numerous studies of the psychology of people in general and of leaders specifically show that there is a beneficial correlation between positive emotions (optimism) and positive outcomes, there's also research that shows that extreme optimism can lead to really stupid management missteps.

"As a leader, your job is to steer and inspire," Jack and Suzy Welch wrote in a *Business Week* essay that argued that leaders who talk about the risk of failure undermine their chances of success. For example, there has been a great deal written about Ford CEO Alan Mulally's ability to inspire workers with his optimistic and hopeful tone. In a story by *New York Times* reporter Joe Nocera, published on May 22, 2009, Ford's chief financial officer Lewis Booth said, "Alan is an exceptionally positive person. In such tough times, people need to see hope, and Alan articulates hope very well."

In April 2012, *Forbes* writer Carmine Gallo described Mulally as "relentlessly optimistic" and noted, "Even in the depths of the auto crisis in 2008, Mulally was the one who always had a smile on his face and a spring in his step. He had a plan, and no matter what happened, he knew that sticking to the plan would lead to positive results." Ford has a strong track record to prove it— Mulally's strategy of focusing on product quality, fuel efficiency, streamlined manufacturing plants, global initiatives, and prizing profits over market share transformed the company.

On the other hand, there have also been plenty of credible researchers, analysts, and businesspeople who have cautioned against the CEO who leads by optimism. "Optimism can blind you to obstacles and lead you to take unwise risks," Norm Brodsky, a veteran entrepreneur, wrote in *Inc.* magazine in December 2011. C. W. Von Bergen and Martin S. Bressler at the John Massey School of Business at Southeastern Oklahoma State University looked at various studies of optimism in businesspeople and found that while confidence has many positive benefits in terms of health and happiness (longevity, faster recovery from illness, fewer people thinking of you as a downer), it has a downside as a business strategy. In their 2011 research paper, "Too Much Positive Thinking Hinders Entrepreneur Success," published in the *Journal of Business & Entrepreneurship*, they wrote, "Extremely optimistic individuals . . . tend to set unrealistically high goals and are often overconfident that they will attain their goals." This, of course, can get you in big trouble.

Sydney Finkelstein, author of *Why Smart Executives Fail: And What You Can Learn from Their Mistakes*, conducted a six-year study across 51 companies and found that executives of failed companies often clung to a distorted and optimistic reality. He noted that these executives typically underestimated business obstacles, observing that "blind adherence to 'positive thinking' became a dominant corporate value that was often at the foundation of organizational failure." Other researchers have found that overconfidence leads to poor decision making that results in lower profit margins, employee firings, and even bankruptcy. There are numerous examples that back these findings. In other words, there's positive thinking, and then there's, "Dude, what the hell are you smoking?"

David Myers, former controller of failed long-distance telephone provider WorldCom, admitted to being overly optimistic about the company's financial problems, which led him to use fraudulent accounting methods to mask declining earnings, telling himself and his nervous staff that everything would be okay. By the time he took off his rose-colored glasses, it was too late: he was arrested for accounting fraud. Oops.

Former Kmart CEO Charles Conaway drove the retailer into bankruptcy and was eventually ordered to pay more than $10 million for misleading investors. The Securities and Exchange

Commission said Conaway failed to tell investors that Kmart was delaying payments to suppliers to save cash, thereby masking the deteriorating financial health of the company. Others felt that Conaway was in over his head, and that the unrealistic expectations were his way of reversing the company's course. Wall Street analysts complained that he "waved too many pom-poms" for Kmart without offering frank data on the actual not-so-perfect state of affairs at the retailer, which led clients to hang up on his investor conference calls. It's fine to be optimistic. It's not fine to be on another planet.

Scott McNealy co-founded the computer technology company Sun Microsystems in 1982. When a recession began in March 2001, business leaders suggested that McNealy cut down on expenses, lay off nonessential workers, reduce research projects, and create inexpensive products. McNealy ignored the advice, believing that the recession would only last a couple of months and would be followed by a strong economic upturn. Optimistic and believing he knew better than Wall Street, McNealy increased expenses and invested heavily in new projects. The recession lasted for nine months, not two, and Sun's sales dropped 48 percent from 2001 to 2004. Its stock dropped from $64 to approximately $4 per share during the same period.

Confused? Is optimism a positive or a negative trait? Let's go back to my friend Jack for a minute—our GHEP, someone who is optimistic about his own abilities but skeptical of the credibility of outside information and people. In contrast, the glass-half-full person (such as Mulally) is optimistic that there are solutions to problems and also understands that the right actions and strategies have to be taken to turn around difficult situations. Academics who study organizations call this "interpretive ambivalence," or the ability to see an issue as both positive and negative. Such people have the confidence to make decisions and follow through on them, changing directions intelligently and nimbly if their first course of action doesn't pay off. In other words, it's fine to be both positive and negative when the situation calls for it.

Want another example of a GHEP? As I've mentioned before, I'm a skydiver in my spare time. Skydiving isn't just about falling out of a plane and landing on the ground. It's about aerial acrobatics: knowing how to maneuver your body in such a way that you can do anything you want with it, knowing when to open your parachute, and knowing how to make it back to the drop zone without injury to you or others. When I jump, I'm optimistic that I'll land in one piece because *I've trained for it*. Would I be that optimistic without having gone through the negatives and without understanding what problems could occur and how to deal with them? Not so much. Optimism is one thing. Blind optimism can get you killed.

GLASS-HALF-FULL PEOPLE ARE PERSISTENT AND DECISIVE

The bottom line is that glass-half-full people (GHFPs) are optimists, yes, but not blind ones. Angst doesn't get in their way, and they also get things done—look at Ford's Mulally. He had a strategy to turn Ford around, and he talked it up to the staff, engaging them and winning their trust and enthusiasm. And then he executed his strategy—made sure it worked and was willing to revise certain actions if they didn't pan out.

Booth School of Business professor Steven Neil Kaplan and two fellow researchers obtained detailed assessments of more than 300 CEO candidates in firms funded by private-equity investors, both buyout and venture-capital firms. They found that execution-related skills—skills like persistence, efficiency, and being proactive—were the most important indicator of the most successful CEOs. "Persistent leaders don't give up. They stick with assignments until they are done. Efficient CEOs get a lot done in a short period of time. And proactive ones are self-directed and regularly bring in new ideas," writes Kaplan. "If a leader doesn't get things done, their employees get frustrated or even leave, particularly the better ones."

Kaplan reminds readers of a best seller written more than 40 years ago, *The Effective Executive*, by the late Peter Drucker, one of the great management thinkers of the twentieth century. His work was based on personal observation, but he came to the same conclusion Kaplan and his colleagues did after completing their more scientific analysis: "Effective executives . . . get the right things done."

Getting the right things done requires a positive attitude, and the inability to make decisions stems from insecurity, fear, and depression. Employees naturally gravitate toward and support people who can make decisions and articulate a rational basis for them. Moreover, when a leader makes and acts on decisions, he or she should be aligned with the business's mission, values, and core principles. What Kaplan and colleagues and Drucker are describing is what I call the GHFP: the person who sees the possibilities and believes success can be achieved but is a realist when assessing challenges.

The glass-half-full leader

- Is enthusiastic about the possibilities but not blind to the problems;
- Is action-oriented;
- Takes time to consider all options and potential results before making a final decision;
- Makes timely decisions and doesn't dither;
- Takes actions that are consistent with business priorities and profits;

- Can articulate logically why decisions are being made; and
- Is balanced in his or her view of work and life.

MILLER TIME

In 1909 the Michigan Star Furniture Company hired an 18-year-old named Dirk Jan (D. J.) DePree as a clerk. Ten years later, in 1919, DePree was named president of the company. By 1923 he had convinced his father-in-law to buy the majority of shares, changing the company's name to the Herman Miller Company. While Herman Miller was never active in the business, D. J. always gave him credit for advocating a policy of quality through the use of the best materials and the best workers.

When a millwright died on the job in 1927, DePree visited the family. The millwright's widow read poetry authored by her husband, and DePree was so moved by this that he made a commitment to treat all workers as individuals with special talents and potential—a story that has become part of the fabric of the company. (As a side note, I'd just like to say what a great person DePree was to do that.)

Herman Miller, like many companies, faced tough times during the Great Depression. Looking for a way to save the company from failure, DePree met a designer from New York named Gilbert Rohde, who argued that DePree needed to move Herman Miller away from making reproductions of classic furniture and toward innovation and products that would suit the changing needs of Americans. DePree took him up on the suggestion, and in 1933 the company debuted a line of modern Rohde-designed furniture at the Century of Progress Exposition in Chicago. Eventually the company also produced the modern and now iconic designs of George Nelson, Ray and Charles Eames, and Isamu Noguchi. D.

J. DePree died in 1990 at the age of 99, but the company has continued to lead the way in modern design.

> "You have to give them a picture of where you're going so they have hope and do the work necessary to get to the other side."
>
> —Brian Walker

In 1994 Herman Miller introduced the Aeron chair. Designed by Bill Stumpf and Don Chadwick, the chair soon became one of Herman Miller's most popular and profitable products. In 1999 it won a Design of the Decade award from *Business Week* magazine and the Industrial Designers Society of America (IDSA). The Museum of Modern Art acquired an example for its permanent collection. During the heady days of the dot-com boom, every start-up executive and wannabe Internet billionaire had one of the iconic chairs—it was a symbol of both power and creativity. According to a June 2006 story in *Fast Company* by senior writer Linda Tischler, Internet start-ups literally ordered them by the truckload. "In late 2000, the company was taking orders for 20,000 to 30,000 per week," she wrote.

But just one year later, the chairs were being listed on eBay for a third or less of their $700 retail price and offered at fire sale prices at dot-com bust office liquidation sales. Like other office-furniture manufacturers who had enjoyed the wave of the dot-com boom, Herman Miller was blindsided by the drop-off in orders once these companies' stocks started to tank and businesses started shuttering their doors.

"We had a two- or three-year period where business dropped 45 percent; that was like an industry heart attack," Michael Volkema, chairman of Herman Miller's board and the company's

CEO in 2001, told *Fast Company*. "In 1995, when I took over, sales were under $1 billion. By 2000, they were $2.2 billion. By 2003, they were down to $1.3 billion. One night I went to bed a genius and woke up the town idiot. It was not a happy time to be in leadership."

Facing what he knew would be a fairly long-lasting downturn, not to mention $56 million in losses, Volkema had to listen when Brian Walker, then the president of Herman Miller North America, told him that painful decisions would have to be made in order to save the company and keep at least some of its workforce employed. Walker knew it could be done, but he also knew that his plan would take a strong stomach and confidence in the market. In late 2001 the executives reluctantly told 4,500 of the company's 12,000 employees that there was no longer any work for them to do. The company also scrapped several promising businesses and sold off more than one million square feet of prime real estate.

Volkema also decided to do something that was seen by both employees and outside observers as incredibly risky, but that he thought was necessary for a brand known for innovation and trendsetting. He invested millions of dollars in research and development that resulted in the development of multifunctional office furniture that nimble companies might find appealing and more products that would engage residential customers. Volkema made his decision based on the perfect storm of shrinking margins and the growth of Chinese manufacturers—two events that wouldn't go away, at least not in the near future. And this decision was in keeping with the core values of the company—remember that during the Great Depression, DePree made a radical decision to go from making period reproductions to becoming a leader in modern design, and it paid off.

In 2004 the company tapped Brian Walker to be CEO. Walker immediately took several steps to bolster morale at the company.

One was to optimistically but realistically convey to staff at the employee-owned company that they shared both the risks and the rewards of the business. According to SEC filings, in January 2009 the company's Executive Compensation Committee and its Board of Directors approved a voluntary reduction of the annual base salary of the CEO and all eight members of the executive team for one year. The base salary for the executive leadership team, except for the CEO, was reduced by five percent, and Walker's salary was reduced by 10 percent.

Walker told *Fast Company* in 2010, "The more open and vulnerable we got as leaders, the more people followed where we needed them to go. . . . You have to give them a picture of where you're going so they have hope and do the work necessary to get to the other side." When employees saw leadership taking pay cuts and suspending their own company 401(k) contributions, it gave them the confidence that Walker and his team had a plan for how to get to the other side.

The furniture maker emerged from the crisis not only financially successful but also with a greater employee commitment to the organization. Herman Miller reported sales of $458.1 million for the first quarter of its 2012 fiscal year, up 20.3 percent from the same period a year earlier. Net income totaled $24.6 million, or 42 cents per share, versus $16.1 million.

Walker's half-full glass just got a little fuller.

SPEEDING PAST COMPETITORS

In a news conference in May 2012, Japanese carmaker Nissan's CEO Carlos Ghosn told reporters that, "despite natural disasters and currency exchange headwinds, Nissan again demonstrated its ability to manage successfully through crisis." The company had just reported that fiscal year net profit had risen 7 percent to $4.27 billion, which exceeded the results at its bigger

Japanese rivals, Toyota and Honda. Its strong showing came despite a devastating earthquake in Japan and flooding in Thailand that both cut supplies of key parts and interfered with vehicle production at factories around the world. In fact, Nissan was the quickest of Japan's three biggest automakers to recover from both tragedies.

> "My kids are very important to my balance, since they keep me informed of what is happening out there in the world beyond my office walls."
>
> —Carlos Ghosn

How has Ghosn, a Brazilian-born executive who does not speak Japanese, run a global company with more than 180,000 employees in a culture that tends to mistrust outsiders so successfully? Ghosn is realistic about his or anyone's ability to predict future consumer behavior accurately, but he's also known for being decisive and prepared to move when consumer behavior shifts. "We don't know where the markets are going, we have to observe what's going down, see the trends, look at every vibration on the market, prepare the technology, and jump when consumers start to think one way or the other," he said.

From January to March 2012, the company posted a net profit of ¥75.34 billion (about $956 million), a gain from ¥30.77 billion (about $391 million) in the same quarter a year earlier. The figure beat analysts' estimates, compiled by FactSet, for a ¥68.5 billion (about $870 million) net profit. Nissan's sales grew across the board in that period, powered by demand for its Serena minivan in Japan, its full-size Altima sedan in the United States, its Sunny compact in China, and its Qashqai small sports utility vehicle in Europe. Ghosn projected revenue to rise 9.5 percent in 2012, beating the previous fiscal year's 7.2 percent increase.

That's nothing; from 1993 to 1999, Nissan global operations suffered seven straight years of losses. Performance was so poor, and forecasts were so dim, that credit-rating services threatened to lower the firm's status from "investment grade" to "junk." At the same time, Asia was in the middle of one of its worst financial crises. In June 1999 Ghosn was asked to manage the turnaround of Nissan, based on his reputation of cost cutting at Renault, a French car company. He agreed and was faced with formidable financial and operational challenges. Shortly after taking on the challenge, in 2000 he became the company's president, and he was named CEO in June 2001.

Despite the challenges he faced, Ghosn showed both determination and optimism that he could turn the failing automaker around. Right after taking over at Nissan, he outlined his plans for the company during a press conference at the Tokyo Auto Show. He explained, with a combination of confidence and accountability, his strategy for saving Nissan and promised that if he and his team didn't achieve the desired results, "my executive committee and myself will resign."

He immediately executed the Nissan Revival Plan (NRP) by cutting costs and increasing revenues at the same time. He turned Nissan around to profitability in less than 18 months and achieved the best financial performance in the company's history. To solve Nissan's problems, Ghosn and his managers had to pay close attention to the opinions of all workers, no matter their rank, and analyze what was being said. "I estimate that a good manager should spend 90 percent of his time listening and only 10 percent speaking," he says.

One key factor in ensuring the success of Ghosn's plan was the creation of cross-functional and cross-border teams, meaning that marketing staff would work jointly with manufacturing engineers and dealerships on projects, instead of working separately and potentially at cross-purposes. "Ghosn is convinced that mixing up the pot will help create value that otherwise would not have been seen or found," says David Evans, a professor at the Reims Management School in France who has studied Ghosn's management style.

Teams are given specific projects as well as the flexibility and resources to actually make progress on them. It turns out to be a smart management strategy. In her book *The Progress Principle: Using Small Wins to Ignite Joy, Engagement, and Creativity at Work,* Harvard Business School professor Teresa Amabile studied what motivates employees and teams to maintain enthusiasm about their work. She found that, more than money, recognition, interpersonal support, or clear goals, employees are most positive when they make progress.

To enhance insight and promote creative thinking, Ghosn, who is famous for putting in long hours during the week, devotes weekends to his wife and four children. "My kids are very important to my balance," he explained in an interview, "since they keep me informed of what is happening out there in the world beyond my office walls. Reading books is another important source of mental nourishment." When you think about it, Ghosn is speaking about *balance,* a key top managerial trait.

Even in fiscal year 2009, a dismal year for most other carmakers (remember those fun little bailouts?), Nissan made a profit. President Obama's administration even tried to tap Ghosn to run General Motors during the bailout, but Ghosn declined the offer in favor of building a Nissan–Renault alliance (just imagine the feeling of turning down a job offer from the president of the United States). "Fiscal year 2009 was a challenging year in the global economy and in the global automotive industry," Ghosn says. "While we have managed through the financial crisis and recession, we have not compromised our strategic priorities. For example, we have not slowed our investments to contribute to a zero-emission society. In 2010, the Nissan–Renault alliance became the first to mass-market affordable zero-emission vehicles [Nissan LEAF]." Vehicle preorders in the United States and Japan surpassed the available production capacity for fiscal year 2010.

Ghosn has many reasons to be cheerful—it's an attitude that certainly works in his and Nissan's favor.

SUMMARY OF KEY POINTS

The glass-half-full person

- Displays courage in the face of adversity;
- Sees the difference between "Everything's ok!" and "Everything *will be ok if we do the following things*";
- Stays inventive and values innovation during tough times;
- Doesn't take bad news personally;
- Doesn't pass the buck or place blame on others;
- Understands that ethics trickle down from the corner office and the boardroom; and
- Rewards transparency and collaboration.

9
TRAIT #7

Customer Service–Centric

"Frankly, you can't be a jerk and be successful in the service business for a long period of time. When you're in the service business, reputation is everything."

—Kenneth Chenault

Customer service happens to be one of my personal passions—all the traits in this book are important, of course, but consumer–business relationships and how they're built are very dear to my heart. In fact, I wrote an entire book about customer service last year, called *Customer Service: New Rules for a Social Media World.* Let me be as blunt as humanly possible: without stellar customer service, *your business will die.* This isn't a fear-based phrase; it's the truth. If you're not focused wholeheartedly on making every customer experience over the top and awe-inspiring, and if you don't drill that mentality down the entire line of your business, your business will die. But here's the funny thing: good customer service is easy to establish and pretty cheap as well—not bad for your most valuable, asset-building calling card.

So why is it so rare? Why must we live in a world where people no longer expect to get excellent customer service? In fact, with each passing generation, the customer service bar is actually *lowered* a bit more. For example, in the 1950s, you could drive into any gas station, and four neatly uniformed attendants would rush over and each handle a different chore, from checking your oil to pumping your gas and cleaning your windows. It was simply *what was done*. Can you imagine that? Four guys, waiting for you to drive in and actually *running* to service you?

I was driving to Atlantic City to give a speech not long ago and stopped to get gas. New Jersey is one of two states, along with Oregon (and the town of Huntington, Long Island—don't ask), where it's illegal for a driver to pump his own gas—its 1949 law banning self-service is still in effect, based on the premise that laymen pumpers could blow themselves up. So naturally, a gas attendant came over. While the gas was pumping, she actually proactively took it upon herself to clean my windows! I was so shocked that I gave her a tip. I can't remember that *ever* happening to me before. But in the 1950s, such service and tips were standard.

Today, service standards stink. Okay, so maybe some people like pumping their own gas or have simply gotten used to it. We've gotten used to a lot of bad service practices, and the worst part is that our typical expectation for a customer service transaction starts out at "poor" and, if we're lucky, ends at "fair." Wonderfully, that's actually good news for you. See, since we have such low expectations of customer service, it's incredibly easy to blow each and every one of your customers' minds and shock them into 100 percent loyalty every single time you're given the chance. All you have to do is simply make sure you and your team treats each customer one level above "crap." Amazingly, you don't even have to be anywhere near great, awesome, or outstanding to be different from the norm. And anything we do that goes above and beyond "one level above crap" is so rare, and so unexpected, that if you do that, you can rule the world.

A 2010 study, "Stop Trying to Delight Your Customers," published in the *Harvard Business Review,* found that customers' loyalty starts to erode when they engage with customer service. Frightening stats include the fact that 56 percent of consumers report having to re-explain an issue, 57 percent report having to switch from the web to the phone, 59 percent report expending moderate to high effort to resolve an issue, 59 percent report being transferred to another person because the first person was useless, and 62 percent report having to repeatedly contact the company to resolve an issue. Study authors Matthew Dixon of the Corporate Executive Board, Karen Freeman of the Sales Executive Council, and Nicholas Toman of the Customer Contact Council found that "loyalty has a lot more to do with how well companies deliver on their basic, even plain-vanilla promises than on how dazzling the service experience might be."

Let me say, then, that the great leader will realize that the first order of business is making sure your team is holding up its end of the social contract. Primal instinct, people—treat customers as if they're paying your salary because . . . they are. Keep your promise simple and stick to it.

THE SIMPLEST ACTS WIN—AGAIN

Not long ago, I received an email from John Korff, president of Korff Enterprises, whose company puts on the wildly popular New York City Triathlon every summer. John has been producing this race for more than ten years, and it's now one of the annual crown jewels of the New York City sports world, right up there with the New York City Marathon and the New York City Ironman Triathlon.

At first, I assumed it was a form letter, since I'd been accepted into my eighth New York City Triathlon. Why so many? Because I'm an idiot who never learns . . . but I digress. I double-clicked to find an actual email, from John himself, congratulating me for getting in again this year and thanking me for doing my eighth one! I was still pretty sure it was a form letter—customer relationship management (CRM) software can easily know those things. But still, it was a nice touch. Either way, I happened to be sitting in front of my computer when it came in, so I dropped a reply back almost immediately to John, thanking him for the note and letting him know that I was also doing the New York City Ironman the next month. Didn't expect a reply, since I still kind of thought I was writing to an auto-email.

Two minutes later—"Wow, Peter—Both! You know, we call those who do the New York City Triathlon then the Ironman the next month 'Hudson Doublers!'" So it actually *was* him. At 6:55 p.m. on a Tuesday night.

What made him email me? Was he looking for repeat "customers," as it were? Those who've completed the Triathlon more than once? If so, it was a smart move—remember, it's not cheap to participate in these races. Perhaps he realized that and wanted to let us know that our continued support of what he built hasn't gone unnoticed. Perhaps he's just *that* nice a guy. Perhaps it was all planned out on a spreadsheet, and it was just my time to get that email?

It doesn't matter. I've run a *ton* of races, all over the place, and this is the first time that any race director reached out to thank me, unprovoked, on his own. You can damn well bet I'm going to race his race every year as long as my body will let me. Another thing that's important to mention. It's not just that Korff is good at sending out emails. Korff's races are very well-run, well-oiled machines of efficiency and organization. I've never gotten pissed off at a race because the staff made a mistake—they do their jobs simply, and they do them right.

Loyalty is built on the little things that you don't really notice when they're present, but that you do notice when they're missing. It's not about upending your customer's expectations, such as delivering a steak to the airport (not that there's anything wrong with that, either, as you'll see). But ironically, I think that's the problem—that's where the disconnect lies for the majority of businesses. We're tricked into believing that the best customer service can *only* be achieved by massive, over-the-top acts of grandeur—the type of customer service events that make the evening news and get blogged about. Those can be great, but as a customer service philosophy? *Wrong!*

I offer you this: the most resonant and effective acts of customer service are the basics that make the customer's life easier. Those are the things that reinforce the customer's loyalty. They can be done daily, usually without any cost except for the cost of training and holding yourself and your team to your standards. Just being "good" fosters customer retention, increases customer satisfaction, and, yes, even grows your customer base by increasing word of mouth through social media and other platforms. In other words: if you focus on getting the basics—starting with humanity and respect—your company will benefit, customers and clients will increase, and, most important, *revenue will rise.*

Don't stop trying to create that one "massive" customer service story that goes viral and winds up on CNN. As long as it does not distract from your core mission to provide basic care, and it is aligned with and reflects your overarching service standards, you never know when you might strike gold. But spend more time focusing on the little things: train your staff to handle problems on their own without asking a supervisor's permission; make sure transactions are as simple and pleasant as possible; say "thank you" when a customer buys your service or product; send the unexpected "we're glad you're still with us" email; make a phone call to your favorite customer to recommend an article he or she might like, and to thank them for being just that (I *love* this one, I've recommended it countless times). You'll be surprised how much of your marketing and PR your customers will do *for* you once you master the basics and come out one step above the norm.

R-E-S-P-E-C-T: FIND OUT WHAT IT
MEANS TO YOUR CUSTOMERS

Loyalty also comes from respect—for a customer's time, money, and business. Remember the unfortunate lesson that Netflix taught us. Once upon a time, the company had red-hot stock and was lauded for its genius concept and ability to deliver on its promise—movies fast, no late fees. Since the beginning of 2011, it has lost nearly 60 percent of its market value because of the terrible customer service mistakes of its CEO, Reed Hastings. It started when he announced Netflix would split its sluggish DVD mail-delivery business from its booming online-streaming business and raise prices at the same time. First, customers were perplexed over the breakup of the two businesses, which felt comfortable together as far as movie viewers were concerned. Hate the DVD you got? No problem, stream a movie instead. Nice. But then it seemed as if that wouldn't be possible without another costly subscription to another costly service. Because what really, *really* made customers mad was the huge *60 percent* overnight price increase. As a result of the abrupt changes and price increases, it was widely reported in the press that the company hemorrhaged nearly 800,000 subscribers in its third quarter.

The backlash was so dramatic that Hastings issued an apology to customers and reversed his plan to split the DVD service from the streaming technology. "I messed up. I owe everyone an explanation," he wrote on the Netflix website. "It is clear that for many of our members, two websites would make things more difficult, so we are going to keep Netflix as one place to go for streaming and DVDs." Hastings did keep the price increase in place, however, which didn't do much to lure back lost members.

The quick apology was needed, but still, it's as if Hastings's customers were an afterthought in the whole process, from start to finish. According to *MarketWatch,* Netflix had a short-lived boost in stock prices in mid-July 2012 but then plunged days later by more than 26 percent. The cause of the decline, according to the report, "was negative reaction to the company's suggestion that it will be a challenge to reach its goal of 7 million new U.S. streaming subscribers this year." Not everyone is down on the company; some analysts suggest buying the stock because it will eventually rebound, but that will come in part from Netflix getting its customer mojo back.

One of the main reasons I currently use a Droid smartphone is because of multiple bad experiences with my old BlackBerry. I was once one of the biggest BlackBerry supporters around, taking the abuse that comes with not having a Droid or an iPhone from all my friends. One of the fun social media sites I use is Foursquare. As one of its first users and an enthusiast, I promoted the hell out of it and became an evangelist because I believed in the concept. But the more I traveled overseas, the more Foursquare wouldn't work on my global BlackBerry. Finally, unable to get answers from either BlackBerry (or Foursquare), I switched to Droid. And now I'm never looking back.

When you're working with consumers, you need to do one of two things: come right out and say there are certain types of consumers you're not going to care about, or care about all consumers equally. Foursquare seemed to be doing the former; unable to get an answer out of them, I moved to a different platform. If BlackBerry doesn't want to work with Foursquare, and if Foursquare doesn't want to support BlackBerry, they both need to come out and say it. That's fine—they're making a corporate decision, one that might piss a few people off, but they're being proactive. They're not sitting there saying nothing. Companies that say nothing are destined, in the long run, to wind up with nothing.

ONE MORE TIME: *IT'S JUST NOT THAT HARD*

CEOs can't run a company from a corner office. It simply doesn't work. For a company to truly embrace radical ways of handling customer service, the entire corporation has to get in on it—and that only happens if they see it coming from the top. Maybe Research In Motion (which produces the BlackBerry) CEO Thorsten Heins and Foursquare's Dennis Crowley don't care that much about being full-service enterprises or about how customers react to their service limitations. In the swirl of excitement over Foursquare's success, for example, that element got lost. Foursquare has to find it, in my opinion, to maintain leadership in the category. BlackBerry has its own issues to deal with. Otherwise, a newcomer could steal their thunder—it happened with AOL mail and many other companies.

When customer service becomes personal, it can have a huge impact on every member of a company. I once heard a story about a CEO driving to a customer's home with a needed part because it came in after hours. I once heard of a CEO who happened to be in the building on a Saturday and answered the phone. The call was a random customer complaining about something. The CEO took the call and got a resolution in 20 minutes—on a Saturday! Both CEOs are well known and very successful, and both run companies known for fantastic service staffs. There's a reason John Korff at Korff Enterprises runs such a successful Triathlon. He cares. He told me that if someone doesn't get into the New York City Triathlon via lottery and emails him, he actually allows the first hundred or so people who email to get into the race. It's little things, whether you are the lucky recipient or you hear the story, that build customer loyalty and trust.

Greg Muender, president of TicketKick, a legal service that helps people fight traffic tickets, works with his team to promote good business practices, honesty, growth, and positive energy, which radiates to customers. When employee issues arise,

Muender always tries to address them with a positive, honest approach and often handles them himself. I love it when bosses step up to the plate personally—you can't do it all the time, but when you do it, it makes a major impact. And talk about karma. In Muender's case, his service model is in stark contrast to other similar companies that often trick customers through loopholes in their terms and conditions and then, when issues arise, blame the customer while simultaneously refusing to help.

TicketKick is determined to do everything it can to please a customer, and, as a result, they are at the top of the field in terms of both growth and revenue. "We virtually have no bad reviews online, and people look at us as the go-to source for traffic ticket defense," says Muender. "People come to us first because we're friendly, we make the process of fighting their ticket easy and educational, and we'll do whatever it takes to help them. We've even gone against our own terms and conditions on several occasions to issue a refund, just to make the customer happy." In the long run, it's not about losing money, it's about losing customers. And happy customers turn into more happy customers in the future—as Muender has proved.

When SPIN! Pizza gets a complaint online, co-founder Gail Lozoff says, "I triage every email and respond to it within an hour or two, and that tends to defuse the guest—especially that personal response. I listen and respond in a way that they know I care and assure them that the manager will be aware of their feelings and use the information to train staff." Gail always asks for customers' addresses so the company can send them some "SPIN! Dough," which can be used to buy a meal. "It's an invitation to give us another chance," she says. The company also holds weekly managers' meetings to share best practices and ways to avoid service mishaps in the future.

Nazim Ahmed, co-founder of Canvaspop.com, the online art company, is obsessed with customer service and as a result has empowered his employees to solve customer problems on the spot—no matter what it takes or costs. "We fix problems so they don't happen again, but my staff has the ability to make a customer happy without transferring them somewhere else, asking permission from upper management, or getting back to them after the fact," he says. As a result, the company has a higher than average rate of returns and referrals. Guys, come on—this isn't hard to do!

Understanding what makes your customers happy and what they care about is one of the easiest, yet most forgotten pillars of customer service. Imagine being able to talk to your audience about issues that relate directly to them when they walk into your store or contact you for an order. Nazim knows that people who order personal art have a strong emotional attachment to the images they send the company to transform into canvases. He makes sure the pictures are treated with that in mind. It's not difficult to achieve. With the level of sharing we're all subjected to on a daily basis, a simple Google alert on your best customers or a perusal of a Twitter account should give you basic insight into what's up in their world. Mind you, I said a quick perusal. There's a fine line between "taking an interest" and "being the creepy stalker who works at Staples."

People also want you to deliver on promises quickly—and I mean that literally. Believe me, we are all sick and tired of hearing a company promise to do something and then . . . do nothing. When something happens the way you were told it was going to happen, it's magical. But that should be everyday par-for-the-course reality. I had a car booked for 8:00 a.m. one morning. At 7:26 a.m., I received a text that my Groundlink car was on the way, and at 7:39 a.m., I received a second text telling me the car was downstairs waiting for me—20 minutes early, just chilling.

When I got downstairs at 7:50 a.m., the car was there, and I was calm, relaxed, and without that rest-of-the-day-killing

"Where the hell is he, I'm going to miss my flight" anxiety that happens when we're on a tight schedule and the car we booked well in advance doesn't show. Can you be like Groundlink? Can you deliver on your promise every time—and maybe even early? Focus on ways to make things happen more quickly. I should mention that customers share personal stories, and that creates more customers. I had a great experience, and I like to share. Guess what: so do your customers.

REMEMBER THE HUMAN TOUCH

You know what was in the Groundlink car when I got in it? A complimentary bottle of water. Simplest thing in the world. The car company probably buys them in bulk at $5 for 20 bottles. That little bottle of water made me so happy. I hydrated and felt just a little bit better when I arrived at JFK. Good luck getting a bottle of water in a taxi. What little things can you do to make a customer feel treasured? What can you do to show them that you recognize that he or she is an individual and that your company is run by people too—people who recognize our collective humanity?

I bought a Keurig machine and some funky flavored coffees for my office/apartment. People actually ask to have meetings at my apartment because they never know what kind of cool coffee they're going to get. I once knew a CEO who went to Africa each year to bring back 30 pounds of a specific type of coffee bean, but he never told anyone where they could get it. His reasoning? "Maybe they remember where they had the great coffee, and maybe they come back for more, and maybe we do some business." (Say that in a Yiddish accent, it sounds much funnier.) But he was right. What unexpected personal things can you do?

I once heard of a metal pipe company that had a corporate customer come in to discuss a new order. While he was there, the customer mentioned to the owner that he had to take a trip overseas because one of his plants was having some kind of problem. Turns out, the metal pipe company also had a plant overseas, pretty close to the customer's plant. The owner of the metal pipe company was able to send his technicians over to the customer's company to fix the problem, saving the customer a $10,000 trip and a week of his life. How loyal do you think that customer is now?

I bet he told his colleagues about that—and brought the pipe company more business. In fact, giving your customers a happy story to tell is a good way of ensuring that happiness is spread (and yes, it's true of bad experiences too—but that potential should keep you on your game). There's a restaurant in the Midwest that has an iPad attached to the bar by the take-out order station. When someone comes in to wait for their food, they're offered a chance to play with the iPad for free. They're also told that if they log into Facebook and "like" the restaurant's page, they'll get a free appetizer, right then and there. The company then thanks each and every customer on Facebook and asks how he or she likes the appetizer. It's a no-brainer, works so easily, and extends the human touch through what is too often cold, automated technology. Perhaps most important, as Facebook starts to ramp up "Places" and "Offers," the company will become the de facto standard for customer experience stories. Why wouldn't you want to help facilitate growth and excitement when the customer is there, in your store, and willing to be talked to? Humans are social. And it's the easiest thing in the world to facilitate.

The customer service–centric leader

- Practices what he or she preaches—attention to service comes from the top: *you.*
- Gives his or her team permission to solve customer problems.

- Makes transactions simple. Do not, I repeat, *do not* make customers work to give you their money. Okay?
- Knows his or her audience. It's not about who you think you are, it's about what your customer thinks.
- Delivers on promises every time, early when possible, and on time when it's not.
- Is unexpected—and therefore happily memorable.
- Isn't afraid to do something truly incredible—and incredibly human!
- Gives customers the tools to tell their story.

A STEAK TO THE HEART

Let me start out with what must be one of the *greatest* customer service stories of all time—and it happened to me (which still blows my mind). I swear on my entire professional reputation and all I hold dear to me that what I'm about to tell you was in no way staged, planned in advance, or faked. It's real and, most important, it's *amazing*. Finally, know that you don't have to do this for every customer. In fact, you can't. But you can do it on occasion, and the payoff will be huge.

When my alarm clock goes off at 3:30 in the morning, I know it's going to be a long day—because it means I'm flying somewhere for the day and then flying home in the evening. One-day roundtrip flights are one of the worst parts of my job, but they are also necessary and, thankfully, fairly rare. One particular morning I had to catch a 7:00 a.m. flight out of Newark, New Jersey, to Tampa, Florida, for a lunch meeting in Clearwater, and then head back to Newark on a 5:00 p.m. flight. It was scheduled to get in around 8:10 p.m., so with any luck, I'd be back in my apartment by 9:00 p.m. or so.

I made my flight and got to my lunch meeting on time. Because of the training/workout schedule I had recently committed to, my first meal of the day was the lunch served during the meeting. It was fine—I had a healthy piece of grouper and a very successful lunch meeting too, which lasted about three hours. By the time I got back to the airport, it was close to 4:00 p.m. Boarding started at 4:30, so I didn't have time to stop for dinner, and I didn't want to grab fast food at the airport. When I got on the plane, my empty stomach rumbled a bit . . . and visions of a steak filled my head.

As I've mentioned countless times on Twitter and on my blog, I'm a bit of a steak lover. Whenever possible, I go out of my way to try steakhouses all around the world, and it's one of the reasons, no doubt, that my trainer is kept in business. Over the past few years, I've developed an affinity for Morton's Steakhouses, and if I'm doing business in a city that has one, I try to schedule a dinner there. I've become a "frequent diner," and Morton's knows it because of its spectacular CRM system. It recognizes me—and my status as a "regular"—when I call from my mobile number. Never underestimate the value of a good CRM system.

Back to my flight. As we were about to take off, I jokingly tweeted the following:

Hey @Mortons – can you meet me at newark airport with a porterhouse when I land in two hours? K, thanks. :)

I had absolutely no expectation of anything actually coming from that tweet. It was a tweet more akin to "Dear Winter, please stop, love Peter" or "Wish I was on Anguilla right now!" I shut off my phone and we took off. Two and a half hours later, we landed at Newark. The fact that a flight got into Newark on time during summer thunderstorm season was a miracle in itself, a detail that will become important in a minute.

I walked off the plane and headed toward the area where the drivers wait, as my assistant, Meagan, had reserved a car to pick me up. I spotted my driver holding a handwritten sign that said "Shankman" on it, so I waved to him and started walking toward the door, expecting him to follow—a routine I've been through hundreds of times before.

"Um, Mr. Shankman," he said.

I turned around.

"There's a surprise for you here."

I turned to see that the driver was standing next to someone else, who I had assumed was another driver. Then I noticed the "someone else" was in a tuxedo. And he was carrying a Morton's bag.

Now understand . . . I'm a born-and-raised New York City kid. It takes a lot to surprise me. *A lot.* I see celebrities on the subway. I see movies being shot outside my apartment and fake gunfire from any given *CSI* or *Law & Order* taping, five days a week. I'm immune to surprises—except this one.

Alex, from Morton's Hackensack, walked up to me, introduced himself, said, "We heard you were hungry, sir," and handed me a shopping bag that contained a 24-ounce porterhouse steak, an order of colossal shrimp, a side of potatoes, one of Morton's famous round loaves of bread, two napkins, and silverware.

> "If there's anything you can say within the social circle, it's that we are communicating with our guests and creating more brand ambassadors."
>
> —Roger Drake

I. Was. Floored.

I never, ever expected anything to come of my tweet other than some giggles and me-too's from followers. Not only that, but Morton's Hackensack is 23.5 miles away from Newark's airport, according to Google Maps. That meant that in less than three hours, someone at Morton's corporate office saw my tweet, got authorization to coordinate the stunt, and then got the ball rolling by getting in touch with Morton's Hackensack to place the order. Then Morton's Hackensack had to cook the order, box it, and arrange a server to *get in his car* and drive to Newark Airport (never an easy task, no matter *where* you're coming from or what time of day it is), and then—and this is the part that continues to blow me away—while all this was happening, someone had to track down my flight, find out where I was landing, and make sure Alex would be there when I walked out of security!

Think about all the things that could have gone wrong: My flight could have been delayed or diverted. I could have exited from a different location. Had I taken the AirTrain and not had a driver, I would have taken an entirely different exit route! Of course, I could have just missed Alex altogether. In fact, numerous other variables could have prevented this customer service caper from coming off without a hitch. I have no doubt that countless companies have a similar thought when an interesting public relations opportunity arises: "Oh, too many logistics. That'll never work," and they leave it at that. But what if it *does work?* What if it happens, and it works *perfectly,* and it shocks the living hell out of the person they do it to? Like it did that night?

And what if that person's first thought was to make it public? Like I did? How long do you think it took me to share what happened, write a blog post about it, and put it all over Facebook? A nanosecond. We live in a world where everyone can be a broadcaster. Do you know *anyone* anymore who *doesn't* have a camera in their phone, or anyone who *doesn't* have a Facebook or Twitter account? Customer service is no longer about telling people how great you are. It's about producing amazing moments in time and letting those moments become the focal point of how amazing you are, told not by you, but by the customer you thrilled. They tell their friends, and the trust level goes up at a factor of a thousand. Think about it: Who do you trust more? An advertisement or a friend telling you how awesome something is? Of course, I immediately tweeted out what happened:

> Oh. My. God. I don't believe it. @mortons showed up at EWR WITH A PORTERHOUSE! lockerz.com/s/130578715 # OMFG!

And sure enough, Twitter lit up like a bottle rocket. The responses are worth reading—here are a few.

kirsten_g
_Tweet@petershankman no joke! That truly is outstanding!! Makes me want to go to @mortons that's for certain!

stephaniegmack
Wow. @petershankman tweets @Mortons w/request for steak on arrival and they actually deliver...to the airport lockerz.com/s/130578715

divahound
_Tweet@petershankman @mortons PHENOMENAL customer service. Way to go above and beyond, Mortons.

rachellaber
Love it! "@petershankman: Oh. My. God. I don't believe it. @mortons showed up at EWR WITH A PORTERHOUSE! lockerz.com/s/130578715 # OMFG!"

rivkaht
Amazing RT @petershankman: Possibly the greatest #custserv story every, and I swear was in no way staged. Thank you, @Mortons. I'm blown away

MsWz
I love it! Thank you for sharing @petershankman -- ::applause:: to you @mortons ;)

My tweet and subsequent blog post about what happened were picked up by a lot of other restaurant, marketing, and business blogs. But for starters, Morton's almost immediately gained

800 followers on its national Twitter account. Roger Drake, senior vice president of marketing and communications at Morton's, explained that because the restaurant knows me so well, when marketing manager Jillian Beard saw my tweet, she immediately reached out to Mike Khorosh, the general manager of Morton's Hackensack, to see not only whether such a delivery could be done, but whether it could be packaged nicely. Mike thought he could pull it off with help from staff member Alex Sariyan.

It's part of Morton's random acts of kindness philosophy, which it employs on a regular basis because the company wants to make brand "ambassadors" out of its customers. "It's indicative of the culture of Morton's going above and beyond every day in restaurants all over the world. If there's anything you can say within the social circle, it's that we are communicating with our guests and creating more brand ambassadors. We do it inside the restaurants, and it translates on Twitter and Facebook with the same level of hospitality," Roger Drake told a reporter from SmartBlog's Food and Beverage sector.

So while you may not consider what Morton's did to be classic "customer service" (fixing a problem immediately, delivering consistently good service and food in the restaurants), it's part of a *culture* of service at Morton's. That means Morton's delivers above and beyond customers' expectations. It practices the conventional service mandates every day—when things go wrong, employees make them right as soon as possible, they make sure that customers get a great steak dinner no matter what location they dine in, and so on. But wowing guests and noticing details by taking a flyer on stunts works well for them too.

There are plenty of marketing gurus and academics who argue against "wowing" customers in order to maintain loyalty and drive traffic. "Stop Trying to Delight Your Customers," the large-scale study of contact-center and self-service interactions mentioned earlier in this chapter, concludes that customers simply want satisfactory solutions to service issues. "Research shows that exceeding . . . expectations during service interactions (for example, by offering a refund, a free product, or a free service such as expedited shipping) makes customers only marginally more loyal than simply meeting their needs," the paper concludes.

But here's the thing—Morton's was strategic and deliberate in "wowing" me. They knew who I was—not simply a loyal customer, but someone who communicates constantly about the things I see in the business world every day. See, regulars are great in the restaurant business, but new customers are even better—and restaurants need both to survive. With that well-choreographed meal delivery, they helped spark a conversation that led to new customers. They indeed created a customer ambassador—me—who not only makes Morton's my first choice in steakhouses, but who can urge a lot of other people to try it too.

Look, if you're messing up customer service left and right, then, sure, one "wow" moment in time is not going to help resuscitate your brand in angry customers' minds. It might even piss them off ("They gave Shankman a steak at the airport, but they served mine cold"). But in Morton's case, customer service permeates the place. Going the extra mile as part of a global service directive demonstrates a keen awareness of how social media make word of mouth a very different animal. Sometimes pulling a rabbit out of a hat, like delivering a porterhouse steak to a weary traveler, is a great, fun way to let people know you take customer service seriously. And it's also a high for the people who work for you—the episode was a big topic of conversation at Morton's for some time and had a positive impact on employee enthusiasm for continued great service.

FULL OF BEANS

American Express and the National Retail Federation (NRF) honor retailers from all sectors that demonstrate superior customer service with their Customers' Choice Awards. The Maine-based sportswear and equipment company L.L. Bean, in business since 1912, has won top ranking in three out of the five years the award has been given and has been in the top ten every year since 2006, a distinction no other retailer has matched. It's won other such awards for service—and its story has been told many times over the years. But iconic brands have lessons to teach, and the way L.L. Bean has adapted its service model to the times and technology without losing its focus and mission—making the customer number one and guaranteeing everything it sells for as long as the owner has it—remains both a remarkable story and a useful one.

The 100-year-old company struggled when the recession first hit but bounced back by 2010 and even managed to grow in the unusually warm winter of 2012. Part of the reason that higher temperatures, which allowed consumers to put off buying down coats and snow shoes, didn't hurt L.L. Bean as much as they did other retailers is that the company expanded its product lines to include more weather- and season-proof items and maintained its level of customer service through thick and thin.

President and CEO Chris McCormick, a 27-year retail veteran, is responsible for nurturing L.L. Bean's service culture, a hallmark the company has been known for since it sold its first pair of duck boots. "Superior customer service has always been and always will be the cornerstone of our brand and is a cultural attribute that differentiates us from the rest of the pack. It originated with L.L.'s 'Golden Rule' of treating customers like human beings, and our service culture has continued to evolve," he told NRF executive director Kathy Mance.

This Golden Rule, devised by company founder Leon Leon-wood Bean, goes like this: "Sell good merchandise at a reasonable profit, treat your customers like human beings, and they will always come back for more." Leon Gorman, L.L. Bean's grandson and chairman of the L.L. Bean board, has famously noted, "A lot of people have fancy things to say about customer service, but it's just a day-in, day-out, ongoing, never-ending, persevering, compassionate kind of activity." McCormick makes it his business to ensure that the philosophy lives on, no matter how much the company might expand or change its offerings and locations.

One of McCormick's ideas that I really appreciate is that you can't just tell customers they'll be satisfied and think that's enough. The customer has to arrive at that conclusion him- or herself, based on the experience he or she has with the company. It's a promise, yes, but it also has to be lived by the person who's buying or returning an item, asking about a product, or solving a problem with something he or she bought. "Our 100 percent satisfaction guarantee stands as a prime example of our service philosophy, since it is all about letting customers define what satisfactory means to them," McCormick says. If a customer says an item is flawed or has fallen down in functionality, it's true—no questions asked. Could you offer that kind of service guarantee?

> "Superior customer service has always been and always will be the cornerstone of our brand and is a cultural attribute that differentiates us from the rest of the pack."
>
> —Chris McCormick

The company conducts weekly online surveys specifically to cultivate rich customer feedback that can be used for continuous improvement. Twice a year, more detailed surveys are mailed to customers that drill deeply into how buyers perceive their service interactions. Of course, online ratings and reviews provide the retailers with a chance to monitor customers' perception of products and shopping experiences and keep track of the pulse of their shopping community. It's a good example of how a very traditional company that sells really traditional (some might say dowdy) clothing and gear stays relevant.

L.L. Bean was able to very clearly understand what was happening with their duck boots when sales went through the roof in 2012. The retailer saw sales of the hunters' and fishermen's staple escalate from 150,000 pairs in 2008 to 500,000 four years later. That spike sent the company into overdrive, hiring more people to construct the footwear and inspiring experimentation with fabric linings and exterior colors like bright blue and pink.

Despite the growth in orders, the new boots were still made by hand in Maine and dunked in a water tank to guarantee their condition-impervious features. And the company still managed to get the orders out the door with the same level of service that has always been in place—that's because McCormick knows how to mobilize his already motivated staff. And after years of hiring scores of seasonal workers, he knows how to pump up an assembly line when necessary. Those are the moments when a company can really mess up and suffer—you know, when Oprah calls and you can't fill orders for the chocolate bonbon she loves so much. . . .

Because L.L. Bean does a tremendous amount of phone sales—Bean catalogs, a tradition since the company's founding, drive most of the company's $1.5 billion revenues—the company makes it a point to provide very personal and prompt phone service. The majority of calls are answered within 20 seconds by a real human being. The company also has staff that responds quickly to emails and online chats, and they make it very easy for customers to comment on and recommend products right on the Bean website.

To ensure that employees fully engage the company's service philosophy, McCormick invests heavily in employee training. One strategy customer service reps employ is to take as much time as necessary to satisfy a customer, answer questions, take an order, and review it. Of course, fulfillment needs to be as fast as possible— but L.L. Bean's staff knows how to be efficient without pushiness. They do not rush customers, as many other sales teams tend to do. Have you ever been on the phone and heard a manager in the background telling the salesperson to speed it up? I have—and it's really annoying. Companies that clock the time employees spend with customers *in order to reduce it* may be doing a disservice to both the seller and the buyer.

Aside from that, L.L. Bean has a Visa program that offers free shipping and free returns shipping, as well as a program that allows shoppers to earn coupon dollars toward future purchases. McCormick recognizes that consumers have become very savvy at shopping across multiple platforms, and as a result, their expectations are higher. "From store pick-ups for online orders to making catalog returns in person, customers want their service experiences to be seamless," he says. As technology opens up new ways of accessing merchandise across the board, making sure Bean customers can get what they want when and how they want it will be a challenge. "It also provides a great opportunity for us to differentiate ourselves in the market. Our goal is to maintain our leadership position for the best customer service," says McCormick. The idea is that no matter how ordering and buying morph and shift—and they will—the company will continue to make service its centerpiece.

SUMMARY OF KEY POINTS

The customer service–centric leader

- Knows that a focus on service builds revenue;

- Puts a premium on what customers say and do;
- Has a structure or framework in place to quickly meet customer demands;
- Works on continual improvement so service problems don't reoccur;
- Changes what's not working without looking back;
- Makes it easy for people to become and stay customers in every way possible; and
- Likes steak (OK, that one's not mandatory).

10

TRAIT #8

Merit-Based Competitor

"The competitor to be feared is one who never bothers about you at all, but goes on making his own business better all the time."

—Henry Ford

On April 24, 2012, American International Group, Inc. (that's AIG, the troubled insurance giant that got $182 billion of our money in the 2010 government bailout) accused Steven Udvar-Hazy, the former CEO of its International Lease Finance Corporation (ILFC) subsidiary, of stealing trade secrets. Udvar-Hazy had left to start his own company after a failed attempt to buy out AIG's aircraft-leasing unit, which leases commercial planes from manufacturers like Boeing to airlines. Following me so far? Good. Anyway, in a complaint filed in California state court, AIG claimed that Udvar-Hazy, along with several former ILFC executives who left to work for his start-up company, Air Lease Corporation (ALC), stole thousands of confidential files that helped the new company establish itself and compete in the marketplace.

Udvar-Hazy, number 330 on the *Forbes* 2012 billionaires list, is an innovator and doesn't seem like the kind of guy who needs to steal ideas. He's widely credited with starting the aircraft-leasing industry and actually co-founded AIG's ILFC unit in 1973. He resigned in 2010 to found and run ALC. The lawsuit said that Udvar-Hazy and other executives downloaded AIG files and "loaded en masse onto ALC's servers" confidential information. ALC has said it plans to fight the lawsuit. "Unable to compete effectively and perceiving Air Lease as a growing threat, AIG/ILFC has now resorted to a baseless trade secrets lawsuit that Air Lease will vigorously contest and defeat," reads a statement from the company.

Also in 2012, office staffing giant Manpower Inc. sued two former executives for allegedly stealing company files, trade secrets, and employees to set up a rival company. In that complaint, Manpower accused former top brass Janis Sonneman and Thereza Chattmon and their new firm, Slingshot Connections LLC, of violating their noncompete agreements, as well as unfair business competition, among other things.

I'm not a lawyer, nor an expert on trade secrets, and I have zero desire to become one. But the story these lawsuits scream out to me is one of misplaced or misguided resources. As of this writing, I have no idea how AIG's or Manpower's lawsuits will turn out, but I can tell you they'll likely be tough to win. According to intellectual property rights lawyers, not only is it difficult to demonstrate the existence of a trade secret and its subsequent theft, but trying to prove it is an expensive and imperfect process. And companies that bring such suits often lose for those reasons.

In June 2012 a federal judge rejected CBS's claim that a new ABC reality show called *Glass House* was essentially a copy of its hit reality show *Big Brother*. CBS also argued that *Glass House* executives lured ABC *Big Brother* staffers to their show and used certain *Big Brother* trade secrets to develop the program. But Judge John McDermott didn't agree with CBS's assessment, saying, "CBS seeks to protect the idea of a show of contestants in a house where cameras are running. You can't copyright that."

Immediately afterward, CBS filed a temporary restraining order to try to block the competing show from premiering, but US District Judge Gary Feess rejected the network's claim, and no restraining order was issued.

Portola Packaging sued rival package maker Logoplaste over Portola's claim that in 2007 Logoplaste was in possession of and used the company's confidential information about its products and customer base. But the argument didn't impress an Illinois state court judge, who ruled that Portola failed to protect its information and ordered the company to pay Logoplaste everything it spent on attorneys' fees over three years of litigation. I guarantee you, that didn't feel good. I don't know how much these two lawsuits cost the companies that brought them, but it's certain they weren't cheap, in terms of either actual cost or time spent on them.

I'm all for companies maintaining the integrity of their trade secrets—if they're actually trade secrets—and I'm also against appropriating someone else's invention as your own. So yes, of course you should vigorously protect your proprietary ideas. I get it. I've been there. Starting new companies that are better and faster and that generate more value than existing companies is in my DNA. The company I founded, Help a Reporter Out (HARO), has been on all sides of this idea. I built HARO because I believed my company could match sources with journalists better than the one company that was doing something similar. It competes with similar services, and other services have been started that try to compete with HARO.

There's one company in particular that I felt was copying HARO's model in a very specific way, which pissed me off enough to challenge them (Want to create something better than me? Go for it, but try not to steal my code in the meantime), but other competitors model their source-matching business differently than HARO, and I've got no complaints about that. Live life, have fun, and create good things. I believe that HARO still matches journalists with sources better than any other service out there, and it continues to develop its functionality, service, and value to stay very competitive. Why not try it—it's free! (http://helpareporter.com)

Here's what it comes down to: it's better and more profitable to compete on merits and strengths than it is to try and take an end run around somebody who challenges you to do better, broadens the marketplace, or disrupts how existing constituencies behave. Why? Simply put, there will always be challengers. Do you really want to spend all of your time in court instead of spending it making better widgets? Nobody can stay in a niche forever—there's always going to be someone who comes into your space and fights to win over your customers. Apple, meet Microsoft, then meet Apple again, for example. Remember, ideas don't happen in a vacuum, and multiple people can simultaneously have similar thoughts and act on them.

Story: Back in 1998, when the horrible film *Titanic* was coming out on video, I took my rent money and had 500 T-shirts printed up that read simply "It Sank. Get Over It." I went into Times Square and sold all 500 in one day. I then leaked the story to *USA Today* and sold thousands of them on the web. Awesome story, right? But in the end, it was simply a T-shirt. I had a moment of glory and moved on. Within four months, there were 30 different websites selling "It Sank." T-shirts. And this was 1998! Imagine how many there'd be if this story had happened today, with CafePress and similar sites all across the Internet.

If you have a solid business plan, be willing to grow it, change it when necessary, and react to the ever-changing customer. Then even if someone tries to copycat you, it's still possible to compete on your merits and win.

Tip: invest more in your R&D and much less in your legal team. I'm not saying don't have a legal team (I personally have the sharpest lawyer you never want to meet), but long-term success depends on striving to continuously improve your product, services, and processes, and continuing to increase the value of what you offer. Go legal only as a last, nuclear option. That's a winning formula. The first rule of self-defense? Have a spectacular offense.

Competing well is not about self-promotion either. End result: no one will ever believe how awesome you are *if you're the one who has to say it!* Every business owner can buy an ad or build a website announcing how great they are. It doesn't mean anything unless it's backed up with demonstrated excellence. Save your money budgeted for ads, put your money into improving your customer service, *and let your customers do your PR for you!* Approach your customers by seeing what they're trying to do that you're good at—and offering some assistance. Show them what you can do—and if they like it, you've started a promising business relationship. The difference between pure self-promotion and an end product or service that is good enough to become its own best promotion is huge. When self-promotion is *seen as help, it's not self-promotion!*

THE "COMPELLING DIFFERENCE" ADVANTAGE

The most positive, productive, and profitable way to compete and communicate your value is by (1) identifying what you're good at, then getting really good at it and making sure your customers know it; and (2) using your strengths to fill needs that the other guys are either too big or too small to serve. What can you do that others in your industry can't do or can't do as well? The book and hardware businesses provide two interesting examples.

What about bookselling? According to Bowker Market Research, Amazon's share of book spending in the first quarter of 2012 was 29 percent, and Barnes & Noble's share of spending was 20 percent for the same period. Independent bookstores account for between 6 and 10 percent of the market depending on which source you consult. The number of independent stores blindsided by big-box discounters and online sellers like Amazon shrank by about 30 percent in the early part of the decade before it stabilized. E-readers reduced sales at brick-and-mortar stores even further. The recession of 2008 didn't help much either—but that circumstance was not unique to the book business. For instance, more than 1,000 bookstores closed between 2000 and 2007, according to federal statistics—today the decline has shifted to "holding steady."

The independent bookstore owners, who see Amazon as a competitor and even a downright threat to their existence, are looking at the marketplace in the wrong way. Their mistake is to focus primarily on price and only secondarily on selection. Few bookstores can compete with Amazon's warehouse facilities and pricing matrix, although some bookstores do match Amazon prices and lower their margins. But ultimately, it's very hard for any business to compete solely on price. Someone can always undercut you, and fighting it isn't worth it—you just don't have a business if you end up giving your product away for free. An independent bookstore might be better off comparing itself to and competing with other local retailers or other local forms of entertainment. Selling books has to be seen as hard-core retailing, not as just a quaint and culturally admirable business.

That might mean changing old business models (there is more than one way for a retail store to sell books) and developing strengths that other stores, or even other means of buying books, can't or don't offer. For example, Suzanna Hermans, co-owner of Oblong Books in Rhinebeck, New York, told *USA Today* that she emphasized personal service and customer relationships, two free rewards programs, physical comfort, the store's popularity as a community gathering spot, and a seemingly counterintuitive system that helps customers order e-books. The store also holds numerous year-round cultural, literary, art, and music events that draw people in. It seems to be working: Hermans added 1,000 square feet to her 2,600-square-foot store in 2011—still small compared to Barnes & Noble stores (an average store is about 26,000 square feet). Because she looks to compete on her strengths and offers something unique to customers, most of whom doubtless buy books from Amazon and other sources as well, the store can flourish. No, Oblong is not a future Amazon, but it doesn't want to be, and that's not the point, is it? See, the idea of competition is to make a profit by offering unique value.

Now on to hardware stores. There are few things that are simultaneously more maddening and frustrating than wandering through one of those badly lit, cavernous mega home centers trying to find a 3/4 screw or a new doorknob set. No one is ever on the floor to help you, and if you do flag someone down, they usually deny carrying the product you want or can't find it if it does exist. A friend of mine, in what was a moment of consumer vengeance and merry pranksterism, once asked a Home Depot clerk where the decorative hose hangers were located. She was standing right in front of them. "We don't carry those, sorry," came the sincere and sincerely lackluster reply. "Oh, I think they're right here," she said as she cheerfully pointed them out. The clerk looked blankly at my friend and walked away. No surprise that Home Depot, despite being the largest home center in the country, often lags behind analysts' estimates for growth and stock prices. Things were particularly rough for the retailer in 2007 and 2008. Still, along with Lowe's, they remain a category leader.

How does a small hardware store compete with the size and scope of big-box home centers? By capitalizing on the qualities that make big-box stores so annoying—it takes a long time to find stuff, clerks are often uninformed, and the stores are not exactly known for appealing displays that make you yearn to get your hands on some mastic and grout and retile your bathroom. You want to get in and out as quickly as possible, but you can't. A smaller store can exploit these qualities. Look at Ace Hardware—I know, it's not exactly your local mom-and-pop shop. It's the largest retailer-owned hardware cooperative in the industry, meaning that mom and pop *could* actually own your local Ace franchise.

Ace's first quarter 2012 numbers look pretty good: revenues of $908.2 million, up 6.3 percent from 2011. The company ranked "Highest in Customer Satisfaction among Home Improvement Stores Six Years in a Row" according to J. D. Power and Associates. Corporate Research International (CRI) has also ranked Ace first in the home improvement retail category for 13 straight quarters based on its "Real People Ratings" consumer opinion survey. These results represent the latest in what have been several years of fiscal health and growth for the chain.

Ace's success is due in no small part to its commitment to offering credible advice from knowledgeable salespeople, selling products in a smaller setting so they are easy to find, focusing its stock on smaller home-improvement jobs instead of huge renovation projects, and displaying items in an old-fashioned hardware store kind of way that makes you both nostalgic and optimistic that you can actually get the job done once you're home. There is something overwhelming about looking at a 15-foot-high stack of lumber—it just makes you want to crawl back into bed. Ace doesn't make the average guy like me, who just wants to replace a hinge, feel that way. Added bonus: I own a condo in New York City. I'll almost always be buying a hinge over lumber.

To tell consumers about their merits, Ace launched an effective and amusing ad campaign that went right to the heart of that issue. The campaign's tagline was very clear about Ace's "compelling difference": Get in. Get help. Get on with your life. "This is part of our re-education of the consumer that we're not a home-improvement store," John Surane, vice president of marketing for Ace, told *Brandweek*. "Our core is about helpfulness and convenience." Ace competes on its strengths and continuously works to maintain the standards it's set and the promise it's made to consumers.

An "independent" hardware store—or any retailer for that matter—can do the same. Tony's Hardware, a small but locally famous emporium on Smith Street in what is now the trendy Boerum Hill section of Brooklyn, has positioned itself on the opposite end of the spectrum from Home Depot. Tony, the man himself, oversees daily what must be one of the only "open box" hardware stores left in the borough—meaning you can pick out a single nail from a bin if that's all you need and purchase it for a few pennies. The guy's got pretty much anything you need in the store, and if he doesn't have it, he'll get it for you the next day. And at about the same price, or often less than bigger stores charge. I mean, come on . . . one nail. How cool is that?

If you have a problem, you can describe it in thing-a-ma-jig and whaddaya-call-it language, and Tony knows exactly what you're talking about, what you need to fix it, and how you should go about doing the job. His many four- and five-star Yelp reviews are a testament to his success at being the "neighborhood hardware store"—and he also has community loyalty to prove it. It's actually the big-box store that can't compete with Tony in terms of convenience (you can walk right over there instead of driving to Home Depot), service, knowledge, or ambiance. That's right, ambiance—the narrow aisles overflowing with tools and doo-dads is pretty much exactly what you want when you live in brownstone Brooklyn and you're looking for a socket wrench. Tony's is good at being Tony's. His uniqueness is a competitive advantage. Focus on being good at being you.

THE PERILS OF COMPETING ON THE WRONG MERITS

Quaker Oats bought the popular sports drink Gatorade in 1983 with its acquisition of Stokely-Van Camp. The buy was

a success and, along with other low-cost food-related acquisi-
tions, actually helped to revitalize Quaker. Because the company
was able to expand Gatorade's geographic market, it managed
to make the iridescent green liquid its top seller by 1987 (today
it comes in numerous psychedelic colors and various other liquid and nonliquid iterations). By 2000 Gatorade accounted for
more than 39 percent of Quaker's sales and operating earnings.
The company continued to carefully broaden distribution beyond traditional supermarkets and convenience stores, successfully penetrating mass merchandisers (like discount stores) and
sporting events, or what Quaker called "points of sweat." Other
sports drink companies weren't serving those other markets as
powerfully.

Yet Quaker could not replicate that success with Snapple, the
brand *Seinfeld* made popular. It bought the brand in 1994 for $1.7
billion. Wall Street analysts sent up flares, protesting that it was
about $1 billion more than the company was worth. Overpay-
ing certainly made it hard for Quaker to compete in the noncar-
bonated drink segment effectively. But the real problem, for the
purposes of this example, is that Quaker brand managers didn't
bring any added value to Snapple in consumers' eyes—in fact,
they seem to have confused consumers by turning away from the
Snapple brand's one-bottle-at-a-time buyer by trying to exploit
mass market supermarket store sales. That strategy sent a mixed
message to consumers.

While Quaker Oats felt confident that it could leverage relationships with supermarkets and large retailers to stock the bot-
tles in large quantities, it ignored the fact that about 50 percent
of Snapple's sales had come from individual sales at small venues such as gourmet delis, convenience stores, gas station kiosks
and "marts," pizza shops, and the like, along with independent
distributors. In effect, Quaker tried to compete on its strengths,

instead of on Snapple's strengths, and it lost. Failing to understand the deep cultural differences between Snapple drinkers and consumers of mass-marketed drinks left Snapple with no competitive advantage. Twenty-seven months after it had bought the beverage maker, Quaker Oats sold Snapple to a holding company for $300 million, $1.4 billion less than they had paid for it. At the point of sale, Snapple had revenues of about $500 million, $200 million less than what it had when it was purchased.

Meanwhile, Gatorade (Quaker is now a division of PepsiCo) has continued to reinvent itself, effectively competing in the sports drink market by continually assessing its most valuable markets and innovating off the drink's energy characteristics to meet its needs. Former Gatorade president Sarah Robb O'Hagan was on maternity leave in 2008 when she decided to dive deeply into the data on the drink, which had in recent years started to lag in sales. The numbers provided a crucial insight. She realized that although the brand was mass marketing to a generic male, aged 18 to 49, the brand's most profitable and loyal consumers were actually much more specific than that: high school athletes made up 15 percent of customers, and dedicated marathoners and weekend-warriors accounted for 7 percent.

Yet those two groups *really* liked Gatorade—that 22 percent portion of customers accounted for 46 percent of all sales, O'Hagan told *Fast Company* in June 2012. Gatorade had to start behaving like a sports performance drink instead of a hangover remedy for frat boys and compete by serving its most loyal and profitable audience. That turned out to be a smart decision—despite a great deal of skepticism from both PepsiCo management and outside analysts. Gatorade and G2 combined posted $1.3 billion in sales in 2011, up 4.1 percent from the previous year. That accounts for a healthy majority of the $1.8 billion sports drink category.

Leaders who compete and excel on merits

- Identify those strengths that customers respond to by keeping track of and examining data and behavior;
- Continually improve on strengths by developing related assets, attributes, and skills;
- Don't seek to destroy competitors but instead find and serve opportunities they miss, ignore, neglect, or simply aren't interested in—what's unprofitable for one business might be profitable for yours; and
- Remember that assumptions aren't facts—look at what's actually happening in your business and in the culture to glean insights into where and how you can compete.

I'LL TAKE A SIDE OF COLESLAW WITH THAT COMPETITION

David Novak is the chief executive of fast-food giant Yum Brands, which operates 36,000 restaurants in 120 countries under familiar brands including KFC, Taco Bell, and Pizza Hut. Novak has led Yum since it spun out from PepsiCo in 1997, first as its president, then as CEO starting in 2000. He added company chairman to his résumé in 2001. The scale of the business is enormous; it generates annual revenue of $12.9 billion. Novak embodies many of the traits in this book—his leadership would have made a good case study in several of my chapters.

For instance, his stewardship efforts have resulted in the company's World Hunger Relief effort, which has generated massive awareness, volunteerism, and funds for the United Nations World Food Programme (WFP) and other hunger relief organizations. To date the initiative has raised $60 million for WFP. Novak has also tuned in to strategic listening. "Our mission is to constantly listen to the voice of our customers, connect with them, and always reach for new innovations and excellence in everything we do," he says.

His competitive strategy, however, is instructive. Despite Yum's size, any leader with any size business can apply Novak's competitive philosophy and tactics. In his book *Taking People with You: The Only Way to Make Big Things Happen,* he wrote, "When I was president of KFC, we had an average customer re-purchase cycle of once every fifty days. Rather than declaring war on our competition, I reframed our challenge, declaring war on that fifty-day cycle and making our step-change goal to envision feeding America a great meal at least once a week."

That reframing resulted in a spate of new and popular products like roast chicken, chicken strips for on-the-go eating, and potpies that could easily be transported and reheated at home—dinner's served. Competition was twofold: KFC competed against itself to increase customer visits, and it competed within the marketplace to develop products that would appeal to people more than what was being offered by other fast-food and take-out restaurants. By developing more chicken dishes that could transition from point of origin to home, Novak worked off the company's strengths and created more reasons for people to visit KFC more frequently. The strategy shaved two days off the average customer-visit cycle, which Novak says represented a big financial win for the company.

> "Our mission is to constantly listen to the voice of our customers, connect with them, and always reach for new innovations and excellence in everything we do."
>
> —David Novak

What has really fueled the growth of Yum has been its global expansion. Interestingly, its KFC brand has shrunk in the United

States and grown overseas. Bringing your assets and skills to new markets and new audiences—places where your competitors haven't yet begun to explore—makes sense. It goes back to the idea of serving needs that others don't understand or don't see. According to a survey of senior executives conducted by the Ashridge Business School, published in its report "Developing the Global Leader of Tomorrow" and presented at the first Global Forum for Responsible Management Education at the United Nations in December 2008, 76 percent believe their organizations need to develop global leadership capabilities, but only 7 percent think they are currently doing so effectively.

Thirty percent of US companies disclosed that they haven't fully exploited international business opportunities, mainly because they don't have qualified staff. Obviously, Yum has the resources and staff development practices to build a lot of new restaurants in many far-flung locations, but the concept can be replicated by anyone. If you want to grow a business, filling empty markets is a smart way to do it, particularly if you see that your original market has reached its natural limit, which seems to be the case with KFC.

According to a March 2012 report in *Bloomberg Businessweek,* investors were enthusiastic about Yum's strategy of selling more fried chicken in China while simultaneously reducing investment in the United States. The magazine's Diane Brady reported that the strategy has had a sustained payoff, allowing the company to increase earnings per share by 13 percent for ten straight years and helping quadruple its stock price. Analysts think Yum can keep the pace going until 2020 and perhaps beyond. There are plans to expand broadly in Africa as well—a plan that dawned on Novak when he visited South Africa and saw people lined up at a KFC franchise. While others assumed there was no market for fast fried chicken in African nations, Novak's in-person observation told him something different. He has virtually no competition in this market—the 660 Yum brand restaurants that have opened in South Africa as of this writing are well positioned to maintain an advantage when other players set up shop.

In February 2012, Novak told *USA Today*'s Kathy Chu that China is Yum's "biggest retail opportunity in the twenty-first century." That is despite the fact that counterfeit KFCs have opened all over the country—because copycats cannot compete with the real thing on merit. The quality controls and consistency built into all KFC operations—and, of course, Colonel Sanders's secret recipe (which is locked in a thick vault at the company's Louisville, Kentucky, headquarters)—mean real KFCs can maintain a "compelling difference" that draws customers. As of this writing, my research hasn't turned up any lawsuits by Yum against the fakers—the company has more important things, like business, to think about.

The key to competing in new markets is observation. It's not enough to just open up shop in a city where your business doesn't already exist. Novak saw that people in Africa were enthusiastic about KFC and had an insight that it wasn't a one-off fluke. I started HARO because, as a PR guy, I saw a need for journalists on deadline to quickly locate individuals who had valuable information to share and saw the same need for small businesses to get their stories out to journalists who cared. There was a platform that was doing something like that—but it was geared toward academics. When a Facebook page I set up to connect writers with all kinds of sources took off, I knew that the idea could sustain itself as a business. In fact, a great number of the entrepreneurial leaders in these pages came as a result of HARO queries. What dots can you connect? What's going on out there that's waiting to be improved, to be tapped, to be fixed, to be made better?

COMPETING INSIDE THE BOX

Tom Crowley, founder, CEO, and president of Illinois-based MBX Systems, started a small business in 1995 selling hard drives to consumers through mail-order ads in computer-enthusiast magazines. The funky little business worked and quickly expanded to include other components. As Internet use increased, the company—then named Motherboard Express—seized on the opportunity to sell its products online.

Motherboard Express proved to be so good at creating PC components that it soon got into the business of building custom "whitebox" computer hardware on demand for clients who wanted something for either personal or commercial use. Many computer professionals prefer whitebox hardware because it is constructed with higher quality components made according to unique specifications, as opposed to the lower cost and quality generic components often found in brand name mass-produced PCs.

Tom was able to successfully compete in this burgeoning market because of high quality control standards, agility in meeting customers' specific needs, and quick turnaround time. Motherboard Express was renamed MBX, and in 2000, it built its first server appliance. When an independent software vendor asked for MBX's help on a whitebox project building the hardware for a new line of server appliances, Tom was eager to get on board. Today, MBX focuses solely on designing, building, and manufacturing server appliances and embedded systems hardware platforms that independent software vendors use to deliver their product. They also offer new product development, branding, and marketing; stocking and inventory management of finished goods; and ongoing support for the hardware and software units it sells. Today, MBX builds for more than 40 different software vertical markets.

The range of competitors that build server appliances is quite varied. For example, Dell has a contract manufacturing division with a variety of predesigned hardware configurations—but it's not their primary focus. Avnet and Arrow Electronics also have original equipment appliance manufacturing divisions, but their sweet spot is selling components. Other competitors that play more seriously in the MBX niche are NEI (Network Engines), AMAX, NCS Technologies, and Iron Systems.

It's a major decision for companies to switch contract manufacturers, because they are often long-term relationships that cover a lot of ground, from the design of the box (branding) and its components to stocking in global distribution centers and supporting their end users' hardware around the world. MBX Systems usually wins this business away from competitors for several reasons. It's known for better-engineered systems with long life cycles (ex-Intel processors change all the time—MBX is proactive with customers' hardware updates); it develops innovative proprietary manufacturing software to handle many complicated custom configurations and orders of all sizes (from six to 600 units or more in one order); it has the highest proven quality in the industry; and it has a short response time when customers need field support such as swapping out a faulty component. It's won several industry awards in consecutive years that back up these accomplishments.

"We respect our competition," says Tom. "They all have a place in the market, and we learn from each other. Our competitive advantage is our focus on supporting software companies, to free them up to concentrate on writing the best software they can without worrying about the delivery system. That's up to us, which is why we think of ourselves as a technology services provider who does manufacturing."

Jill Bellak, president and COO of MBX, says the company "looks at the market as a whole. If our competitors are doing well, that means the entire market is healthy, which is good for us. If our competitors are not doing well, that's likely to affect us too at some point." The fact that the field of competitors is definable gives Jill and Tom an opportunity to really look at prospects closely and determine whether their current providers are meeting their needs, or if MBX would be a better fit. If they conclude that a prospect would be better served by MBX, the executives are in a very good position to make an informed case to a company to make a switch. "We've found there to be a real bottom line advantage in being honest about our strengths and our competitors' strengths—and how they may or may not work for potential clients," she says.

"Our largest competitors are very good at scale, and that appeals to customers that don't need a lot of specializing but a manufacturer that's very good at doing the same thing multiple times. Our small competitors are whitebox builders who will do anything for anybody but can't do it with consistency or quality," says Jill. As a result of this analysis, MBX takes a "middle of the market" approach—servicing fairly large and mid-sized customers who have a degree of volume but also need some specialization and custom features.

> "In our business the mantra is, anything we can do to make a client's job easier than anyone else can is of utmost importance."
>
> —Jill Bellak

"The secret sauce is that we invest heavily in internal software development," says Jill. "We have software developers in house who write custom software to manage production internally, and it's been an effective competitive strategy because our own software breeds efficiencies that our competitors aren't capable of."

Despite the fact that the International Organization for Standardization inspectors (the IOS sets international requirements for quality management systems) who come to look over the production line always marvel at MBX's manufacturing software and have even suggested that Tom market the system to other analogous businesses, he sticks to doing what MBX does best. "Lures like that might sound tempting, but they can distract us from our mission," he says. MBX in-house software has resulted in 99.5 percent defect-free workmanship, an impressive record.

"As a product moves through the manufacturing line and goes to work centers where various tasks are completed, the software will not allow the builder to sign off on a task until the system detects that all the details have been taken care of," says Jill. "The second piece of our effective quality control is culture," says Tom. "Everyone understands that in order to be successful, we need to deliver a product that does what it's supposed to do. That's a priority. There are hundreds of things that could go wrong from start to finish, so to maintain the quality in the various platforms, people have to be focused and they have to care. Those are defining qualities of our staff." It has to be—MBX does not do spot-checks, which is a common practice of other manufacturers. Every product is individually inspected multiple times. It is an investment that has paid off—MBX has a 98 percent customer-retention rate.

Tom also invested in building a robust customer portal where clients can share feedback with service reps, obtain detailed information about orders, ask questions, and make suggestions. "The response when we show a prospect this system is genuine amazement; they tell us they've never seen a service system that provides a similar amount of information and ease of use," says Tom. "Internal software development has been such a benefit for attaining and retaining business, and that's why we continue to look at and invest in our internal software team as an integral part of both new business development and customer support."

Managers and leaders are viewed in an "upside-down" fashion—meaning their role is to serve everyone else and make sure staff has exactly what is needed to get the job done right. There is a tremendous amount of cross-pollination between the internal engineers and product developers, customer reps, line workers, and management. The team that works on internal systems, for example, is fully integrated into the company and not socked away in some corner only to come up for air during holiday parties. So if a new warehouse system is being developed, an engineer spends time working the warehouse so he understands those employees and how their jobs could be improved. "They can then go back and write something that will be successful," says Tom.

Finally, MBX does quarterly business reviews with customers. "In our business the mantra is, anything we can do to make a client's job easier than anyone else can is of utmost importance. That's why we make sure to be very competitive on quality. After all, the client is putting its name on the boxes we manufacture—our name is not on the line in the same way," says Jill. "I had a customer say to me, 'To be honest, it is my relationship with my account manager Kristin that I value the most. I feel she works for me without being on my payroll; calling her is no different than calling someone down the hall. I know she is going to do her best for me and my company.'" If a customer feels that strongly, why would he or she leave?

Think for a minute how you could compete by being more nimble, responsive, customer-centric, and quality focused. How could you make your business more effective at engineering capabilities for customization or ease of use?

ENTERPRISING COMPETITION

Andrew Taylor, CEO of Enterprise Rent-A-Car, says the business's success as a brand leader comes from its focus on customer service, something it is widely recognized for—Enterprise has been ranked highest in customer satisfaction for seven consecutive years in the J. D. Power and Associates' North America Rental Car Satisfaction Study. The guiding philosophy of the company, which was started by Taylor's father, Jack, more than 50 years ago, says that every interaction with a car renter, from the start of a reservation until a vehicle is returned, is regarded as an opportunity to please and gain a lifelong customer.

That's why Enterprise is often featured in discussions of customer service excellence. I could have easily put the company in my section on service, but Enterprise also competes on its merits, which is a leadership commitment of both the current CEO and his father before him. Andrew Taylor has also admitted that he's "constructively paranoid" about competition and, as a result, flies hundreds of hours a year to visit branches in a very hands-on approach to managing the business and proactively looks for ways to appeal to customers, who do have a choice.

For instance, early on, Enterprise kept costs down and cars accessible by avoiding airports with high rents, which had to be passed on to the consumer with higher car rental fees. The company made a decision to locate storefronts primarily in real neighborhoods, which put cars closer to the people who needed them—those who had to rent a vehicle while their own car was being repaired and those who wanted to rent a car as a means of traveling for both business and pleasure. It was smart both competitively, because other car rental agencies weren't penetrating into urban neighborhoods or close to residential areas, and economically, because it meant that Enterprise could, in fact, compete on price. Of course, now, since Enterprise has such scale, you can also find them in close proximity to airports, usually a short van ride away.

Taylor told *Investor's Business Daily* that a proprietary technology developed in house helps insurance providers reduce the number of days a rental car is needed following an accident. You might think that doesn't make business sense for Enterprise, since it cuts down on rental fees. The longer a rental agency can keep a car in the hands of a car owner, the more money it makes, right?

"In fact, when we save our partners money, they bring us more business," said Taylor, and his strategy proved to be right. Many insurers prefer Enterprise, and it gets a lot of their business.

Because service is a centerpiece of its "compelling difference" that has become so attractive to customers, Enterprise has to work very hard to maintain a high level of service excellence. With more than 7,600 rental locations across North America and Europe and more than 68,000 employees companywide, that can be a challenge. Enterprise operations are largely decentralized, and managers are given a great deal of trust and autonomy to run their branches as if they were their own businesses. In 1989, Enterprise Rent-A-Car had a 66 percent customer-satisfaction rate—that's how many renters said they loved driving Enterprise rentals.

I can think of a lot of company leaders who would be more than happy to take that 66 percent and run. But Andrew Taylor didn't think it was so great. He was COO of Enterprise at the time, and he thought 66 percent looked pretty low. Taylor wanted to move the satisfaction level up the scale substantially. At first, it didn't quite work out that way. In 1994, three years after becoming CEO, the satisfaction level had actually degraded and was at 60 percent—and competitors were starting to encroach on Enterprise business. Taylor didn't particularly want the business to constantly focus on finding new customers over maintaining repeat renters. "It costs five to six times more to gain new customers than to keep current ones, so repeat business is crucial," according to Kirk Kazanjian, author of *Exceeding Customer Expectations: What Enterprise, America's #1 Car Rental Company, Can Teach You about Creating Lifetime Customers.*

Then Taylor came up with a way to not only measure but also improve customer satisfaction—meet the Pavlov's dog of customer service management. Local and regional managers could forget about promotions unless they excelled at customer service.

For a performance reward system to work, there had to be a way to measure and designate a customer service score so managers could see for themselves how they were doing.

"In fact, when we save our partners money, they bring us more business."
—Andrew Taylor

The company developed a Service Quality index (ESQi). Each month thousands of customers are asked two questions: 1) On a scale of one to five, how satisfied were you with your rental experience? and 2) Would you rent from us again? Each rental location earns a ranking based on the percentage of customers who say they were completely satisfied with their last rental experience at that rental agency. The scores for local operations are compared with a corporate average and play a major role in decisions about employees' rewards and advancement. "So, for example, even if a given location is profitable, if their ESQi number is not at or above the company average, that manager cannot be promoted to the next level on his or her career path," Taylor told J. D. Power.

Taylor also competes by giving customers services they want but don't consistently get from competitors, and he finds out what those services are by analyzing feedback from both managers and customers and taking suggestions from both seriously. "In fact, it was one of our employees who first came up with the idea to pick our customers up when they're renting from us, and now we are known throughout the travel industry for that added level of service," says Taylor. No one in the rental space does this. Enterprise attracted customers by making the idea memorable through its famous ad line, "We'll pick you up." The company has also innovated other service benefits, like adding fuel-efficient and alternative-fuel vehicles to its fleet, implementing a WeCar car-sharing program, Rideshare vanpooling, and hourly car rental.

More recently, Enterprise started conducting brand integrity audits. Assessors who work for the company visit its airport locations and evaluate customer service; bus service and condition; counter, return, and exit booth service; brand image; facilities and wait times; and, perhaps most important, vehicle cleanliness and condition. If you've ever rented a car and found (and smelled) a half-eaten cheeseburger and fries in the back seat like I have, you know why this last bit is so important. Both Alamo Rent A Car and National Car Rental brands adopted the audits after Taylor acquired them in 2007.

Enterprise buys 7 percent of the cars made in the United States, making it the biggest car buyer in the country. Other car rental firms sell the cars and trucks they buy back to the manufacturer after a year or two, and then re-selling them becomes the carmaker's problem. Taylor decided it would be more competitive to sell the cars directly to consumers. It would also be riskier, but there was an opportunity to make better margins on the sales and bring in different kinds of customers. Selling cars to individuals would bring them a better price than they would get from selling fleets of Fords back to Ford and so on. It was a smart move—people can get great deals on virtually new cars, and Enterprise controls its assets in a financially beneficial way. For example, in fiscal year 2011, the company sold 65,000 cars directly to consumers and the rest as wholesale to car dealers.

I admire the way Enterprise defines service as their "compelling difference" and as a result defines what service means very broadly—anything that makes the customer experience easier, faster, and more valuable gives them a competitive edge. It's the three taken together that makes Enterprise's competitive strategy work so well.

SUMMARY OF KEY POINTS

Leaders who compete on merits

- Observe the marketplace and examine data for competitive insights;
- Provide customers or clients with new reasons to return;
- Customize what they do or how they do it to make the customer experience memorable and personal;
- Find new, fun ways to make change work;
- Grow by meeting needs of new or unserved markets; and
- Build loyalty through unique characteristics that create value—what makes you, you is a competitive advantage.

11
TRAIT #9

Gives a Damn

"Leaders are people who do the right thing; managers are people who do things right."

—Warren Bennis

Of all the traits in this book, "Gives a Damn" may be the most natural to come by, because it is in great part instinctual. It's also the easiest trait to lose when leadership responsibilities become broader and more complex. How you respond to internal or external critical situations—and how the response filters down to those who work for and around you—is an essential clue to the value you place on integrity, ethics, and honesty. Before I invest in a company, for instance, I'm interested in looking at many "bottom line" issues, such as management, processes, and long-term growth potential (I invest in companies to make money; I donate to charities to help their missions)—but I also look to see whether a company's leaders promote ethics and humanity because, in my experience, those companies are better positioned to offer the most shareholder value. Giving a damn goes beyond stewardship—it's bringing personal integrity to your professional obligations.

Bernie Madoff obviously didn't give a damn—and you can see where that got him. But giving a damn isn't easy either—doing what you know to be right can sometimes have a devastating effect on your career. It takes a tremendous amount of grounding and character to overcome the temptation to say, "Screw it, it's not worth the fall out" or "There's no profit in acting on this" when you see something troubling. Those are the moments when leaders are either made or broken. Turning down the easy buck to instead do the right thing is one of the hardest choices we have to make.

HOUSTON, WE HAVE A PROBLEM

Roger Boisjoly was an engineer with NASA supplier Morton Thiokol in the 1980s and was a key player in the story of the *Challenger* space shuttle disaster. He died on January 6, 2012, at age 73 in Nephi, Utah, near Provo—although his passing didn't make national obituary desks until nearly a month later. You may or may not remember the details of the *Challenger* crash, but they're worth taking a look at again.

It was January 27, 1986, one day before the *Challenger* space shuttle was about to take off from the Kennedy Space Center with six accomplished astronauts on board, along with "the first teacher in space," Christa McAuliffe. Boisjoly went to his supervisors to warn them for the last time that the spaceship's O-rings had serious flaws that would be compromised by the unseasonably chilly weather—the thermometer had dipped below freezing overnight, and weather predictions indicated that the cold snap would last at least into launch day. And in fact, it was damn cold the morning of the launch.

Boisjoly had outlined temperature effect on the O-rings six months earlier in a detailed memo to the same superiors. In it, he warned that cold weather would cause the seals connecting sections of the shuttle's huge rocket boosters to fail. "The result could be a catastrophe of the highest order, loss of human life," he wrote. That's why on a cold Florida day in January, he and 14 of his colleagues begged their bosses to postpone the takeoff. But NASA was pressuring the company to go forward with the launch—it was a public relations goldmine that had been building for months. That, and the fact that Morton Thiokol depended financially on NASA's $400 million annual contract, ultimately led the managers to dismiss Boisjoly's advice. He could not bring himself to watch the launch, so sure was he that it would end badly. Seventy-three seconds after takeoff on January 28, the *Challenger* exploded, killing all seven crew members as their families watched in horror.

The memo Boisjoly wrote was made public soon after the disaster—and it was a bombshell. He became known as a whistle-blower during a federal investigation of the explosion. Many hailed him for doing his best to stop the takeoff from happening: Boisjoly was awarded the Prize for Scientific Freedom and Responsibility by the American Association for the Advancement of Science, became an active speaker on corporate ethics at universities and in front of civic groups, and was in demand as an expert on forensic engineering.

However, he also paid the costly bill that whistle-blowers often incur when they speak up. His company, Morton Thiokol, demoted him and another engineer who had also vigorously warned of the danger, moving them to a less prestigious area of the company that wasn't involved with space work. William Rogers, chairman of the presidential commission that investigated the disaster, noted, "It would seem to me . . . they should be promoted, not demoted or pushed aside."

Colleagues and managers also shunned him. According to a 1987 interview with the *Los Angeles Times,* Boisjoly described a one-time friend telling him, "If you wreck this company, I'm going to put my kids on your doorstep." The scientist also reported suffering from posttraumatic stress syndrome, depression, double vision, headaches, and occasional outbursts of anger.

Even though the investigation by the presidential commission placed the blame for the faulty O-rings squarely with Morton Thiokol, Charles S. Locke, its CEO at the time, took a defensive line, saying, "I take the position that we never agreed to the launch at the temperature at the time of the launch. The *Challenger* incident resulted more from human error than mechanical error. The decision to launch should have been referred to headquarters. If we'd been consulted here, we'd never have given clearance, because the temperature was not within the contracted specs."

But if that were true, then why didn't the managers feel comfortable going straight to Locke with Boisjoly's critical information? Why did the managers who pushed aside Boisjoly's warnings keep their jobs? No one was fired. And why, after hearing Boisjoly's testimony on Capitol Hill, did Locke say, "People are paid to do productive work for our company, not to wander around the country gossiping." In May 1986, Locke told a *Wall Street Journal* reporter, "This shuttle thing will cost us this year 10 cents a share." Later he complained that the remark had been taken out of context. It may well have been—editing to change meaning has certainly been known to happen more often than it should in journalism. However, in October 1986, the *Chicago Tribune* reported that Locke had no plans to resolve any friction that might remain between company engineers and managers who clashed in the wake of the shuttle explosion. When a reporter asked Locke whether he should resign in the wake of the explosion, he replied, "You explain to me why I should." You can't make this stuff up, can you?

The *Challenger* didn't explode because of a poorly designed O-ring alone. It crashed because of a decision-making system that reflected Locke's corporate ethic, which may have enabled

NASA's Marshall Space Flight Center tradition of discouraging bad news. Patrick Moore, PhD, a professor of English at the University of Arkansas at Little Rock, has written extensively about institutional communication failures surrounding the *Challenger* accident, including his 1992 paper, "Intimidation and Communication: A Case Study of the *Challenger* Accident," published in the *Journal of Business and Technical Communication*. "For two years, I taught at the University of Alabama at Huntsville [where NASA's Marshall Space Flight Center is based] a few years after the *Challenger* accident. I mentioned *Challenger* from time to time in my technical communication classes while there," he says. "One day, one student said she had been an intern or student worker at Marshall, and she had seen an interesting poem on an engineer's bulletin board. You can see from it how the NASA hierarchy at Marshall did not like bad news, and how they suppressed it." The NASA culture of the time was one of intimidation, confused communication, and "fatal politeness," says Moore.

This ethos infected NASA managers and is the critical reason they turned a blind eye to the serious problem that resulted in the *Challenger* disaster. In Morton Thiokol's case, it seems that the company's financial performance and the client's interests (and pressure) took precedence over public and project safety. Profit first, and second, the lives of seven astronauts, and the image of smoke trails circling back down to Earth forever seared in my mind and those of thousands of other schoolchildren as we watched that fateful launch.

The second point about this story is that Charles Locke, who went on to oversee Morton International when it split from Thiokol, made money for shareholders, retired as chairman in 1994, sits on boards, and seems to have lived happily ever after. I don't know Mr. Locke, and I also understand that he came of age at a time when the world was very different for CEOs. I do argue, however, that he would have had a much harder time surviving as

CEO had such an event—and his reactions to it—happened today. Sure, there was plenty of newspaper coverage of the *Challenger* accident and criticism of Locke. But two things didn't exist then: the skepticism of corporate CEOs that abounds today, and the immediate audience that today's connected world brings to the debating table seconds after a problem occurs.

It goes precisely to my original argument—in today's transparent world, someone like Boisjoly could have and probably would have tweeted his concerns about the O-rings to his followers if his superiors ignored his advice. Then there would be inevitable retweets, and reporters would investigate. Reporters would be tougher on Locke and NASA managers today—they would be held to a higher standard fueled by skepticism. In Locke's case, it's because shareholders are much more active today than they were in the 1980s. "In the corporate raider days back in the 1980s, shareholders were quick to grab almost any offer that was higher than that day's stock price. But today's shareholders are sadder and wiser," according to Nell Minow, editor of Corporate Library, a research service specializing in corporate governance. "Shareholders want more than a couple of dollars a share. They want leadership they can believe in," she wrote in a *Chicago Tribune* op-ed.

Boisjoly was the *true* leader at Morton Thiokol. The hair on the back of my neck stands up thinking of how differently events would have turned out had management at the aerospace company heeded the word of one of their best troubleshooters. What do you think you would have done in the same situation?

Have you created a culture of humanity—where you speak the truth and want to know the truth in return? Does your business take character and integrity seriously? Do you have a system in place that takes crucial information from a variety of sources seriously? The most effective leaders I know care not just about business, but about the people who are part of it and impacted by it. They see that their work is part of the larger picture, conscious that the stones they throw in the pond every day as they make decisions create ripples beyond their sight lines.

IS IT ME, OR IS IT HOT IN HERE?

In late September 2011, the *Morning Call,* an Allentown, Pennsylvania, newspaper, and the *Seattle Times* both published investigative stories about heat conditions at local Amazon warehouses. Elmer Goris, for example, explained to the *Morning Call* that he had spent a year working in the Pennsylvania warehouse but had to quit because he could no longer stand the often 100+ degree Fahrenheit temperatures.

Goris, 35, had worked in warehouses for more than ten years but had never dealt with anything quite as physically harmful. During a heat wave, he became ill. Goris saw a co-worker pass out and paramedics arrive to carry overcome workers out of the warehouse in wheelchairs and on stretchers. Paramedics, at the request of Amazon, parked in ambulances outside, ready to treat workers who suffered symptoms of heat stress. Those who couldn't quickly cool off and return to work were sent home or taken to area hospitals. Employees who couldn't keep up with the pace were fired, reports said. Employees from the Seattle area told the *Seattle Times* that they had sustained injuries on the job and had been pressured to seek treatment discreetly, so the government wouldn't be alerted to potentially unsafe work conditions at the warehouse.

After Amazon workers complained about working conditions to federal regulators, Occupational Safety and Health Administration (OSHA) officials inspected the warehouse and shortly afterward issued recommendations to Amazon about how it could improve the way it handled heat stress. After the news broke, shareholders weren't pleased. Despite the fact that the company had been experiencing a record boom in business, the complications involved in fulfilling orders efficiently opened the door to potentially dangerous ramifications for workers, which could result in nasty fines, not to mention fatalities. At the shareholder meeting the following year, in May 2012, company CEO Jeff Bezos told the audience that Amazon planned to spend $52 million—a drop in the bucket for the mail-order giant—to retrofit its warehouses with air conditioners.

Amazon may be giving shareholders great value—but if the media hadn't reported on the story, and if employees hadn't alerted OSHA to heat-related workplace hazards, what would have happened to its stock price had there been fatalities at the warehouses? Would shareholders have felt that efficiency requirements that pushed staff to work beyond their physical limits and produced cost savings on energy were really worth an extra dollar or two on the stock price? Are poor working conditions, the kind that you associate with Chinese sweatshops, a fair exchange in return for a job? I'm not sure that this is how the enlightened self-interest of capitalism is supposed to work. Are you?

Does Bezos give a damn? He touted many stewardship and charitable projects at the 2012 meeting—all admirable. But many shareholders were more concerned that he reverse potentially dangerous working conditions at the company's warehouses. If people are unable to work, products can't be delivered, and customers will revolt. Ergo, shareholders aren't going to be getting much value. For that reason alone, it's enough to give a damn about the temperatures in your warehouse. You see how giving a damn isn't about unprofitable altruism. There's a reason for it that even Adam Smith, that early proponent of free enterprise, understood. Treat your workers well, and your customers will be the real winners.

ANSWERING THE CALL

Leaders who cultivate companies full of people who give a damn impress the hell out of me. When employees at every level of an organization feel comfortable and confident enough to express random acts of humanity, it offers important clues as to the quality of leadership at the C-suite level.

When Hurricane Katrina's fury devastated New Orleans, Dr. Patrick J. Quinlan, CEO of New Orleans–based nonprofit Ochsner Health System, along with many other Ochsner employees, provided uninterrupted service during the hurricane—it was just one of three hospitals in the area that remained open during the storm. Ochsner pathologist Dr. Gregory Henderson was in the French Quarter when the storm hit. He treated New Orleans police officers in need of medical attention and was the *only* doctor in the Convention Center surrounded by thousands of desperate people—yet he maintained his calm and provided care however he could.

Ochsner employees also managed to keep the only operational pharmacy in the city open for the first three days after Hurricane Katrina so that patients with chronic illnesses such as asthma and diabetes could continue receiving their life-saving drugs. Workers protected the blood supply and kept lab supplies safe and sterile during power outages and other setbacks during and after the storm. In addition to providing for the city's health care needs, Ochsner hospital administrators found a way to issue paychecks without electricity to more than 8,000 employees. Warner Thomas, president of Ochsner Health System, said this was all possible because the company had an effective disaster plan for employees. It is also a tribute to the value both Thomas and Quinlan place on their constituents—the people of New Orleans.

I occasionally browse reddit, a social news website where registered users submit news items, many of them local. Other members, called redditors, vote on how much they like each story. It's a good source of interesting local stories that you don't find from a daily scan of other news sites. One of my favorite reddit stories was posted in 2010. A member wrote that her 89-year-old grandfather was snowed in after a blizzard hit the Wayne, Pennsylvania, area. He didn't have a lot of food on hand, and he lived alone, so after talking to him on the phone and hearing about his predicament, his daughter called around to the local supermarkets to inquire whether any delivered groceries.

After several no's, she finally found one that would deliver: Trader Joe's in Wayne. As a policy, Trader Joe's doesn't actually make deliveries. But the employee who answered the phone was willing to make an exception for the World War II vet—plus it was the holiday season, so why not? Great! The woman placed the order and mentioned in passing that her dad was on a low-sodium diet. The TJ employee recommended adding a few low-sodium products to the order, and the woman agreed. They delivered a few days' worth of food within 30 minutes of receiving the call. Moreover, the store didn't charge the family for the delivery—or the food. "The funniest part is now my grandpa is trying to leave his apartment in the snow to thank them, but I think we've stopped him," wrote his granddaughter in a follow-up post.

Underneath the posting, a string of many other tales of Trader Joe's staff's (called crewmembers) generosity appeared. Plus there was a message from Trader Joe himself! "Hello redditors! Thank you for your kind words. We are not quite sure which employee did this, but we will be in contact shortly so that you can personally thank him/her. We encourage this type of service at all our locations across the states. Thanks again for your kind words!" And then later the post was updated: "The person in question is a little hesitant to have their name on the Internet. Send thanks to: 171 E. Swedesford Rd, Wayne, PA 19087."

Okay, there is no Trader Joe, and I'm fairly positive that even though CEO Dan Bane is known to spend two to three days a week in stores bagging groceries, greeting customers, and talking to them about what they like or don't like, he didn't actually write the note either (given that I corrected a few misspellings in it, and he's got more important things to do than reply to reddit postings), but *somebody* in the company was paying attention.

Retail is a tough business, and food sales can be even more challenging. But as grocery store work goes, Trader Joe's seems preferable over other alternatives. Writing in the *Huffington Post*'s feature "Food Informants," a crewmember named "Jane" wrote, "I like working for Trader Joe's because they pay me well and offer great benefits. They also respect me as an employee and make me feel like I'm useful and needed and not just another part-time employee that can be replaced (which has been the case at other retail jobs I've had). Trader Joe's is really good at hiring great people, and I'm lucky to have so many wonderful co-workers."

According to a story in *Fortune* magazine, crewmembers aren't given margin information on products, so placement decisions are made based on what's best for shoppers in specific stores and not on profits per unit. The privately held and very private company has roughly $8 billion annual sales and makes twice as much as Whole Foods does per square foot (and with cheaper prices). Part of that success comes from production and ordering efficiencies, low prices on high-quality products, and the resulting customer loyalty. People love their Trader Joe's. I would also argue that the store is successful because on some level Bane encourages compassion—instead of getting pissed off that a crewmember gave away food, the company commended it and did so publicly. (They also have a robust food-donation program, which is part of the company's stewardship practices.) That's give-a-damn leadership.

Thomas J. Falk, the chairman and CEO of Kimberly-Clark, practices give-a-damn leadership on an impressive scale—you can (and should be able to) do that when your global sales are about $20 billion annually. After the February 2010 8.8-point Richter scale earthquake hit Chile, Kimberly-Clark, through its nonprofit partner MedShare, the Kimberly-Clark Foundation, and Kimberly-Clark Latin American Operations, sponsored the shipment of a large container of medical supplies to Las Higueras Hospital in Talcahuano, Chile. Kimberly-Clark Argentina donated one million diapers for the youngest disaster victims through five different local nonprofit organizations; Kimberly-Clark employees in Chile also volunteered their work time to relief organizations in the area to provide assistance to those in need. The company had previously brought tremendous aid in the form of both funds and products to Haiti after a 7.0 magnitude earthquake in January 2010 and to Asia after the devastation caused by the tsunami in late 2004. You can find information about these efforts on the corporate website, but when help goes out, the company's PR department doesn't simultaneously pick up the phone to call reporters.

It's not my intention to sound like an advertisement for Trader Joe's or Kimberly-Clark, or any other company for that matter. You can complain about the sourcing practices that allow Trader Joe's to sell lemons and other products so cheaply, and you might have a legitimate beef; likewise, you may see the environmental impact of disposable diapers as a blight on Mother Earth, and no doubt there's some truth in that concern too. I simply want to point out that where you find an earnest attempt at integrity, you also find success.

Giving a damn means:

- Doing what you *know* is right—even if it means scrapping a costly project or turning down a lucrative-sounding deal;

- Listening to bad news and weighing its ramifications honestly;
- Understanding that your company isn't an isolated organization, but part of a community—and behaving accordingly;
- Knowing that while you have to provide shareholder and/or stakeholder value, it shouldn't be at the cost of exercising basic human decency and integrity; more important, doing the latter will usually provide the former; and
- Engendering the spirit of giving a damn among all employees.

DOING WHAT MATTERS WHEN IT COUNTS

Great leaders earn their reputations in times of crisis, not during times of prosperity and tranquility. Is there a CEO in the world who could have truly been prepared for the tragedy that occurred when New York was attacked by terrorists on September 11, 2001? Kenneth Chenault, CEO of American Express, was on a business trip in Salt Lake City when the World Trade Center collapsed right across the street from American Express headquarters at the World Financial Center. Eleven American Express employees who worked in the neighboring towers died in the attack. When Chenault heard the news, he immediately called the AmEx security team, located in the company's headquarters, and had them evacuate the building—in contrast to the security team at the Twin Towers, which had initially advised people to stay in the buildings after the first one was hit.

Thousands of company employees were stuck in Lower Manhattan—bridges and tunnels were closed to vehicles, and only foot traffic could travel in and out of the city that day. Because air transportation had been halted, hundreds of thousands of AmEx cardholders were stranded in cities, towns, and airports around the world. According to an account of Chenault's actions that day in *PR Week,* the CEO empowered his customer service team to help the 500,000-plus marooned cardholders get home in any way possible. The company even chartered planes and buses to help people reach their destinations. AmEx also waived late fees and extended or increased credit lines to help customers cover the cost of travel.

Nine days after the attacks, Chenault stood in front of almost 5,000 AmEx staffers at Madison Square Garden in New York and personally consoled grief-stricken employees. Chenault also announced that the company would donate $1 million to the families of the 11 AmEx employees who died. According to reporting in *BusinessWeek,* Chenault "demonstrated the poise, compassion and decisiveness that vaulted him to the top."

"Leadership is also obviously very important during challenging times. When I talk about leadership, I often think of something Napoleon said: that the role of a leader is to define reality and give hope. Now, I don't want to wind up like Napoleon, but this is the simplest definition of leadership. In 2001 I tried to communicate to the organization the reality of the situation we were in. You've got to tell people the hard truth, that there are difficult actions that you must take, and what the consequences are of those actions," Chenault told *Bowdoin* [College] *Magazine.* "However, you must also provide reasons for why people should be hopeful. A reason for hope that I communicated to our employees during 9/11 was that American Express has been around for more than 150 years, and we'd faced many crises during this time, including wars and natural disasters. Every time, the company dealt with the crisis head-on and emerged even stronger, more resilient."

Although the travel industry was hit hard immediately following the attacks and for several months afterward, Chenault managed the company through that difficult period. He told *Money* in October 2001, "We've got to face reality, but we can't get mired down in reality." In May 2011 he recounted the experience before a group of 75 emerging social sector leaders at the American Express Leadership Academy, telling them that in order to get through a crisis, "the key is to balance decisiveness with compassion. You cannot be afraid to make the tough choices, but you have to do it in a compassionate way."

Chenault did face serious issues after 9/11, as he had in the spring before the attacks took place, when he had to write off more than $180 million in bad junk bonds he had inherited from his predecessor; in July 2001 he had to take another $826 million write-off. Quarterly income plummeted by three-quarters in the aftermath, AmEx stock price dropped by half, and 14,000 staff members had to be let go. Three months after the attacks, AmEx revenues from its travel business had declined by two-fifths, which resulted in the painful elimination of 6,800 more jobs. By 2003, AmEx stock had significantly recovered, outperforming the S&P 500 and doubling its stock price from what it was immediately after 9/11. In 2007, *Fortune* magazine named AmEx one of the nation's "best companies for leadership development." Flash forward to the first quarter of 2012, when net revenue was $7.6 billion, 8 percent higher than in the first quarter of 2011, according to its shareholder report.

Chenault's compassionate management philosophy helps AmEx stay flexible and innovative—which is hard for a company of its size (it's an international conglomerate that employs more than 80,000 people) and in its industry (financial services firms aren't generally known for their warmth and fuzziness). For instance, it has heavily invested time and resources into a robust social media platform, and it is constantly innovating to make the consumer experience not only more rewarding and economical, but also more profitable for the company. Its advanced employee health care program with on-site care facilities also represents a substantial investment. This program benefits the company by keeping employees healthy and productive. At the end of the day, like any public company, AmEx sees its commitment to shareholders as priority number one. "I want to win every day in the marketplace," Chenault told *US News and World Report*. "I want people to say that Ken Chenault is a person who, while he's focused on winning, [does so] with the highest level of integrity."

PERMISSION TO BE COMPASSIONATE AND USE COMMON SENSE

Kim Jeffrey is president and CEO of Nestlé Waters North America Inc., based in Stamford, Connecticut. He oversees the largest bottled water company in North America, with 7,500 employees, 30 plants, and more than 100 facilities. Mr. Jeffrey joined Nestlé in 1978 as a central division sales manager and advanced over the years before assuming the company's top position in 1992. With sales of $4.4 billion in 2011, the company holds seven of the top ten US brands, including Poland Spring, Arrowhead, Deer Park, Ozarka, Zephyrhills, and Nestlé Pure Life. In fact, Nestlé Waters North America commands a 35 percent market share of the bottled water category in America, with a 42 percent share of the polyethylene terephthalate (PET) single-serve segment (PET are clear, tough bottles with excellent gas and moisture barrier properties), which is the largest and fastest-growing aspect of the bottled water business.

It's tough to be in the bottled water business today—those ubiquitous containers are a constant target of environmentalists and others who feel they are ruining the planet even though bottled water serves an important function in terms of emergency water storage and travel. But Jeffrey is a realist, and he gives a damn about the environment: the company has been a leader in building Leadership in Energy and Environmental Design (LEED) plants certified by the US Green Building Council, reducing water and energy use, and preserving 14,000 acres around more than 50 spring sites for watershed and wildlife protection. Other major initiatives include reducing raw material usage and advocating for modernized recycling systems to increase reuse of existing plastic packaging. As part of his personal commitment to the environment, Jeffrey co-led the Nature Conservancy of Maine's historic Campaign for Conservation, which helped protect more than 185,000 acres of the wild St. John River.

My writing partner, Karen, didn't know squat about this when the planes flew into the Twin Towers on September 11, 2001. She was trying to get home, along with everyone else, on that horrible, fateful day. She walked home from Midtown, all the way to Brooklyn. It was hot and sunny. It's about six and a half miles between East 42nd Street and downtown Brooklyn. "We were all tired, upset and relieved, and sweaty as we finally made it over the Brooklyn Bridge," she says of hundreds of other people who made that trek with her. "But when we got to the other side, there were all these young people lining the streets, and they were handing out cups of water."

Karen noticed that the water was being poured out of big containers marked Poland Spring. "How the hell did Poland Spring mobilize so quickly?" she thought as she looked at those kind faces. "Transportation was halted, no one was getting into the city or across the bridges." Still, there they were, these amazing kids making sure anyone who wanted it could have as much water as he or she needed. As it turned out, the company's water trucks were the only nonemergency and nonofficial vehicles that got through the Lincoln Tunnel, to bring water in, after the disaster. Set this against stories that emerged days later of small stores gouging people for water, charging two or three times what it normally costs—not an urban legend. True.

"After that, I kept looking for stories about Poland Spring in the newspaper," says Karen, yet she could not find a single one. Certainly, despite the tragedy, a company would capitalize on the fact that they had done a good deed. There was zip. "I actually wrote a letter to the *New York Post,* which they published, after a story came out about a coffee chain that had done a distasteful ad shortly after 9/11 showing a firefly careening into two large cups of iced coffee. People felt the joke wasn't funny," she says. "I wanted people to know what I had experienced from a company that seemed to care, without the requisite publicity seeking afterward."

So we were both pretty curious to know how Nestlé's brand Poland Spring was able to mobilize so quickly and get not only water but also a team of volunteers out to Brooklyn to distribute it where people badly needed it. The story is told here for the first time. When Karen told Jeffrey she's now a lifelong Poland Spring water customer, you could tell it made him slightly uneasy, because it's clear that winning customers was not the reason the company's employees got water out to the public that day. Still, there's a real sense of pride in his voice, knowing that what those employees did had such a personal impact.

"Nothing came from this office telling employees to distribute water," he says, "but I am not surprised it happened. We've been disaster relief partners with the Red Cross for 25 years." As Jeffrey points out, there are three things people need immediately after disaster occurs: shelter, water, and then food. "Our employees doing that on the spur of the moment is a result of how we push responsibility down as far as we can. We make the assumption that our people are smart enough to know the right thing to do, and then they do it. When you go to a drugstore to make a return, the person needs some other senior person to oversee or approve it, even though the person you are talking to seems perfectly capable of making the decision and carrying out the return process.

That's not how we see things. You do not give the keys to the store away, but for the most part, I want people to feel well thought of enough to make and carry out decisions like responding in an emergency with something we have that people need."

The story is that a key Nestlé Poland Spring distribution ware-house is located in the Brooklyn Navy Yard, not that far from the Brooklyn side of the Brooklyn Bridge. "I am sure that employees called friends and family and said, 'Can you get down here and help us give out this water?' We have a culture that gives people the autonomy to make decisions that are also in sync with com-pany values. We want inspired leadership at all levels. What hap-pened [on 9/11] was completely spontaneous—it's not something I had requested, no one asked for permission—[and] since we have great people who have and are encouraged to use common sense, and great systems in place, it's also very doable," says Jeffrey.

"Great systems" is an understatement—in fact, the company has more route trucks in Manhattan than Coke does. Some of the company's trucks were actually offered to and commandeered by emergency workers to help at the site, and gladly, too. "We lost a bunch of trucks that day—I do not even know how many were destroyed," says Jeffrey. And he doesn't care. "We didn't lose any people that day—we had people in harm's way who we managed to get out of the way."

Shareholder value is certainly on Jeffrey's mind in all this—it has to be; he has an obligation to investors, after all. "The inter-esting issue is how we measure it," he says. "In an Internet society, a company's reputation can be ruined in 24 hours, so making deci-sions on myriad issues has to involve considering how we conduct ourselves, as well as the companies we do business with. Anyone who ignores reputation does so to their peril. Especially when you work with a product that has a humanitarian function. A lifetime of good works has insulated us from the idea that 'bottled water is bad and you can't have it.' There are people who believe this, but the vast majority agrees that what we do enhances shareholder value. I have never had any shareholder or stakeholder come to me saying I am doing something wrong."

Jeffrey also maintains robust succession planning and 360 evaluations, through which employees (including Jeffrey) can get a view of their performance from peers, subordinates, and superiors. "I did not create the system," he says, "but it helps mature people from a business standpoint to develop more quickly—the value of operating this way invests them in the mission of the company, and it facilitates a symbiotic relationship with them. You can't get the best out of people if your corporate values do not match the way they would live at home. I want people to feel comfortable to speak their minds if they think something isn't right. It takes a long time to create a culture where it works, but the teamwork and effort that came out of 9/11 shows you it's time well spent, an investment worth making."

The company's decision making can be summed up in a simple, but pretty effective way. You always choose openness over fear, and you can never ignore the reality of your own situation. When you make a decision, you have to think about whether you want it on your tombstone. "We can be pressured by situations to go with the flow and do the wrong thing when you know it's wrong, and I would submit that this happens all the time," he says. "There are red, green, and yellow lights in life, and as executives, we know what red means and what will happen if we ignore it. We know you can't sail right through a yellow light without slowing down and pausing. When you make decisions, what's the impact on other people?"

Thanks to Jeffrey, his division maintains a rule that if someone proposes a policy that disrespects 95 percent of the people, it's a no-go. Fair decisions benefit the bulk of the people every time and not just a lucky few. You can make decisions every day based on the short term or on how they will look on this week's

P & L. But you can't just operate on a technical level alone; you have to deal with the human element. Executives who win realize that they need the passion and commitment of employees, and they institute practices that make people happy. Maybe that's why Nestlé has been nonunion for decades—that does not happen where trucking is involved unless workers are happy.

"It may be a generalization to say so, but I do believe life is a marathon," says Jeffrey. "In the marathon, the nice guys do ultimately finish first, even if the other guys win a sprint." Hear, hear.

SUMMARY OF KEY POINTS

Give-a-damn leaders

- Make decisions based on shareholder value and impact on corporate integrity;
- Do what's right, even if it's not always obviously profitable—because they know that real profits come from doing the right thing;
- Ask for, expect, and consider the opinions of stakeholders and experts;
- Accept ultimate responsibility for the global impact of decisions made at every level of the company; and
- Create avenues for employees and stakeholders to share concerns without fear of reprisal.

CONCLUSION

NICE GUYS (AND GALS) ARE THE FUTURE OF BUSINESS

Once upon a time, I helped the iconic singer Tony Bennett with some public relations work for a nonprofit he was involved in. The one thing I remember more than anything else from my time with him was what a gentleman he was. He would, without fail, stand up every time a woman got up from or returned to the table, or whenever a woman walked into the room. He had old-school manners, and it made quite an impression on me. One of my longest relationships was with a woman who wasn't even going to accept the offer of a second date, she revealed to me later, until I did two things that changed her mind: I asked about her day, and I stood up when she got up to go to the ladies room.

What do these anecdotes have to do with leadership and success? Tony Bennett, after all, doesn't run a Fortune 500 company or have thousands of employees working on broadening his musical strategy. On the other hand, after serving in World War II,

Bennett developed his voice and with Columbia Records sang on many albums and had numerous hits throughout the 1950s and 1960s. He had a tough time personally and financially getting through the rock-and-roll years, but he staged an extraordinary comeback in the late 1980s and 1990s, connecting to a young audience without having to sacrifice his musical style for current trends.

As of this writing, Bennett is still going strong as a concert performer and a recording artist. He has won 17 Grammy Awards, including a Lifetime Achievement Award, and two Emmy Awards, and he has been named an NEA Jazz Master and a Kennedy Center Honoree. His records have sold more than 50 million copies worldwide. That qualifies as some kind of quality leadership, don't you think? And his success is all because he stands up for a woman when she gets up from a table.

Okay, it might be a little bit more than that. It's what those manners represent: Tony Bennett is a nice person. He also thinks constantly about his career and music and tries to make good decisions that will benefit his bottom line. There's no way he could have made it through the changing tides of musical taste, a crumbling marriage, and drug addiction and back to superstardom and prosperity if he were a jerk and completely disregarded the norms of honesty, integrity, and fair play—the three unspoken governing rules of enterprise.

As for me, well, I learned that being truly interested in and respectful of a date and being a stand-up person in business have quite a lot in common. It's behavior that keeps you grounded in reality. Ultimately—and this goes back to my core message— being a selfish bastard who doesn't believe the rules apply to you simply won't get you very far.

You see, the rules *do* apply to us. As I've said from the start, the world is moving quickly toward a place where people want and expect to know who they are dealing with when they enter into commerce of almost any kind. As communication becomes more fluid, leaders will be more exposed. We won't be *able* to hide anything anymore. The world will demand that CEOs improve their ability to articulate why they make decisions. The best way to defend capitalism and entrepreneurism is through a fair exchange (or good services for compensation) that encourages repetition of the same. If part of that exchange necessitates that you behave in a professional manner, than you'd damn well better act in a professional manner. Whatever the parameters of your exchange system are, stick to them, and you really don't have a lot to worry about. By the way—you should also know that this isn't limited to corporate behavior. It applies everywhere. A rule to live by.

In closing, I want to offer a few simple tips that I've found to be useful for new or hopeful leaders who are building their credibility and reputation, and that may serve as reminders to people who have been leading for a while. It's easy to forget the small stuff. It never fails to impress me when I see a leader of any kind treat a waiter or a clerk in the same way he or she would want to be treated, with deference and respect. The first businessperson known to quantify lessons of success was probably William Julian King, known as W.J., a one-time General Electric engineer who retired as a UCLA engineering professor in 1969 (he died in 1983).

His little book, *The Unwritten Laws of Engineering*, made an impression on Raytheon CEO, now also chairman, Bill Swanson. He took King's lessons and added some of his own, creating a booklet of 33 short leadership observations, which he called *Swanson's Unwritten Rules of Management*. Raytheon employees have given away more than 250,000 copies of the little book. Included in that version is the truism about waiters: "A person who is nice to you but rude to the waiter is not a nice person. (This rule never fails.)" Do you know why executives take potential hires out to lunch? Because they want to see how the person treats the waiter. I can't tell you how true this one is. I've not hired people because of their attitude toward waiters, busboys, or even taxicab drivers.

"Watch out for people who have a situational value system, who can turn the charm on and off depending on the status of the person they are interacting with," Swanson writes in his version of King's book. "Be especially wary of those who are rude to people perceived to be in subordinate roles."

I have a few rules too—and that's what I'll leave you with.

1. **Exceed relatively low expectations.** Sure, it's awesome to set the bar really high and exceed it. And I'm not saying don't do that. But focus on building your reputation piece by piece. If you really don't want to follow up with a person you've just met, don't suggest a future coffee date as a throwaway "nicety" when you bid them farewell after your first meeting. If you DO want to have coffee with someone, why not suggest a Skype call, and when you email to follow up, upgrade it to coffee? Start off low and grow quickly. It's the easiest thing in the world to do.

2. **Do "unexpected follow-up" daily.** I have a big, big stack of business cards—probably more than 4,000 cards. These are people I've met once, usually at a conference or trade show. They're not "contacts" per se, but they're also not complete strangers. I keep these cards in a giant fishbowl on my desk, where people who don't constantly worry about their weight would keep candy. I worry about my weight. Business cards are calorie-free, even if you eat them. Each day, I pull ten cards out and email the lucky winners, just to say hello. No selling, not even that much talking about me—just asking about them. How are they, what are they working on, etc. This keeps me

"top of mind" and does two other things: It brings some of those people from "quasi-contacts" closer to "clients" or helpful members of my network. And, as an added benefit, it makes me first in their mind when someone they know asks if they know anyone who does what I do. Another bonus? I get to say hi. Nice touch.

3. **Find out what people are doing.** If you had any idea how many people I have Google alerts on, you'd call me the king of stalking. But, in fact, those alerts are one of the most helpful tools in my arsenal. Someone gets quoted? Drop a congratulatory note. Someone gets promoted? Send cookies. Someone takes a new job? Send a six-pack. It is not hard, doesn't cost a lot, and keeps you well above the fold of mediocrity. Why? *Because no one else does it.* Everyone wins! (Especially you!)

4. **Pay attention.** This is probably the simplest one to say, yet the hardest one to implement. Think about it—when was the last time you listened to someone talk and actually comprehended what he or she was saying, as opposed to waiting for a break so you could start to talk? The thing about a conversation is, it takes actual work. It's so much easier to listen while nodding your head and checking your BlackBerry or wondering what you're going to do for dinner. But at the end of the day, that won't help you. *Listen to what someone says and make notes about key points.*

Ask about those key points later, or follow up on them down the line, and you separate yourself from the rest of the people your new friend talks to on a daily basis. *Know when to shut up.* You see these people all the time in meetings. They talk to hear themselves talk. They have no good ideas, and no one wants to be around them when they start prattling away. They're never invited to parties, and they rarely get promoted. So often the best thing you can do for your reputation is to simply shut up and listen.

5. **Separate yourself from the pack.** The pack is stupid. Accept that and be better than the pack. That means doing things like your mom (and Tony Bennett) taught you. Someone older than you? "Sir" or "ma'am" never hurts. Be the person who makes the introductions. "Sam, have you met Michelle? Both of you are into gastrointestinal research." You've become, at the very least, the connector and, at the best, the person who gets to take the bow when Sam and Michelle start a new venture together or get married.

6. **Keep a mirror-image bag at** your office or any other place that you spend the most amount of time after your home. A mirror-image bag will have enough necessities to get you through 48 hours of extended away time. A suit if you wear them, a freshly pressed shirt and pair of jeans if you don't. Toothpaste, toothbrush, soap, underwear, socks, and—important—aftershave or perfume. Check out Three Fluid Ounces (www.3floz.com) to buy tons of small-sized mirror-image stuff. One of my favorite scenes in *True Lies* is where Arnold Schwarzenegger gets out of his wetsuit, dons a tuxedo, and has a little compartment for cologne. You always want to be the person most put together in a situation where no one expects to have to be put together. This gets you remembered, not simply recalled.

7. **For God's sake, if you do nothing else, just be nice!** A smile goes a hell of a long way toward proving you're not full of shit. Just by being a touch nicer—offering to help someone put his or her bag in the overhead compartment, letting the obviously time-crunched person go ahead of

you at Starbucks. . . . You never know where these small, innocent acts can lead, but do know this: if they lead anywhere, they start off with the other person believing you're different from everyone else—and from there, it's up to you to keep proving that.

Have fun. Life is meant to be lived, and we're meant to be nice people while living it. It's a fun ride if you do it right. I want to know what you think, and I answer all my own emails (another trait). I'm at peter@shankman.com. Let me hear what you have to say.

And hey—thanks for reading.

INDEX